Song of my life

Books by Harry Mark Petrakis

NOVELS

Lion at My Heart
The Odyssey of Kostas Volakis
A Dream of Kings
In the Land of Morning
The Hour of the Bell
Nick the Greek
Days of Vengeance
Ghost of the Sun
Twilight of the Ice
The Orchards of Ithaca
The Shepherds of Shadows

SHORT STORY COLLECTIONS

Pericles on 31st Street
The Waves of Night
A Petrakis Reader: 27 Stories
Collected Stories
Legends of Glory and Other Stories
Cavafy's Stone and Other Village Tales

MEMOIRS AND ESSAYS

Stelmark: A Family Recollection
Reflections: A Writer's Life, a Writer's Work
Tales of the Heart: Dreams and Memories of a Lifetime
Journal of a Novel
Song of My Life

BIOGRAPHIES/HISTORIES

The Founder's Touch: The Story of Motorola's Paul Galvin
Henry Crown: The Life and Times of the Colonel
Reach Out: The Story of Motorola and its People

SONG
of my life

a memoir

HARRY MARK PETRAKIS

THE UNIVERSITY OF SOUTH CAROLINA PRESS

© 2014 Harry Mark Petrakis

Published by the University of South Carolina Press
Columbia, South Carolina 29208

www.sc.edu/uscpress

Manufactured in the United States of America

23 22 21 20 19 18 17 16 15 14   10 9 8 7 6 5 4 3 2 1

Library of Congress Cataloging-in-Publication Data
Petrakis, Harry Mark.
Song of my life : a memoir / Harry Mark Petrakis.
pages cm
ISBN 978-1-61117-502-8 (hardback) —
ISBN 978-1-61117-503-5 (ebook)
1. Petrakis, Harry Mark. 2. Authors, American—
20th century—Biography. I. Title.
PS3566.E78Z46 2014
813.54—dc23
[B]
2014032721

This book was printed on a recycled paper with
30 percent postconsumer waste content.

Once again, perhaps for the final time,
to my beloved Diana, love of my life

CONTENTS

1

Beginnings

In the summer of 2011, for the first time in almost a year, I rode the South Shore train from my home in northwest Indiana into Chicago, a distance of about fifty miles. The downtown terminal, for years called Randolph Street, had been extensively remodeled and renamed Millennium Station.

I have traveled this same route back and forth at least several hundred times in the nearly five decades since we moved from Chicago to Indiana. On this trip into Chicago I read without paying attention to the landscape. On my return journey from Chicago, I stared out the window at neighborhoods I had often observed before. I found this journey different. In some inexplicable way I seemed to be viewing the South Side of the city for the first time.

Some of this altered perception came from obvious differences in the terrain. The South Loop, which for decades had been dotted with the bleakly identical high-rise buildings of the housing projects, had those buildings demolished and replaced by glittering glass and steel condominiums to house the gentry.

Further south, the train entered the community of Hyde Park. Before Diana and I married, this was the neighborhood where she lived with her family. We courted along these streets for several years, strolling the grassy expanses of Jackson Park and sitting on the stone pilings of the promontory at 55th Street. As we gazed across the lake at the misted Indiana shoreline, we never imagined that the later years of our life would find us gazing from Indiana toward the skyline of Chicago.

On a bench in the shadow of the imposing Museum of Science and Industry, with its classical Greek statuary, I had kissed Diana for the first time.

A few blocks North of the Museum on East 53rd Street, my father-in-law, John Perparos, had his cleaners and shoe repair shop. I can never think of that good loving man without recalling his pledge to me before his daughter and I married.

"My boy, I have no dowry to give you, but this promise you have. For as long as I live, your clothes will be cleaned and pressed and your shoes will have new soles and heels."

SOUTH OF HYDE PARK, the train entered Woodlawn, with its cramped yards and decrepit garages behind small frame houses. The arabesque of stairs and porches suspended on the back of two- and three-story apartment buildings were identical to the ones I had ascended and descended so many times as a boy.

Sitting across from me in the train and adding to my resurrection of the past, was a young family of four. The husband wore jeans, sneakers, a baseball cap and a jacket, while his pretty blonde wife was dressed in slacks and a jacket. They had two blonde boys of about five or six who looked identical enough so that they might have been twins.

The boys played quietly with small toys. The husband gazed at the floor of the train while his wife stared pensively out the window. I sensed each one secluded in their own thoughts, a certain divide between them. That feeling of separation might simply have reflected their weariness after a day in the city with small children. Seeing that family made me recall the years when my wife and I with our young sons rode the train to and from downtown Chicago.

I wondered how the period of a few months since my last trip on the South Shore could have produced such a marked change in my perceptions of the city. Perhaps in old age (I have been an octogenarian for nine years now) the past refocuses and our impressions are noticeably altered, as well. In his epic, *The Iliad*, Homer wrote, "When an old man is concerned in a matter, he looks both before and after."

If a year could have produced such an alteration in my perceptions, I considered the lengthy span of time that now separated me from my youthful years. Although I have written extensively in the past of my family, my childhood and adolescence, my marriage to Diana and the birth of our sons, as well as my early efforts to write and publish, those remembrances had been penned decades earlier.

If my view of the city where I grew up could have so changed in less than a solitary year, how might those impressions of my earlier years when I lived nested with my parents and siblings, have changed? As human beings, hair, body, muscles, organs are changing all the time. It is only reasonable to assume that with these changes must come altered perceptions as well. Perhaps in reviewing the past I will see essential obligations I have left unfulfilled. Some of these commitments may still be redeemable, but I understand others will forever be lost. Even God lacks the power to change the past.

So now, as a consequence of that brief train journey, I will burrow once more into the cloisters of my life, exhume the spirits of those I loved. I will revisit the neighborhoods of my youth; call up the visages of old friends and in Homer's words, "Look both before and after."

Perhaps at this advanced stage of my life, a reappraisal of my past will allow me to recast these memories in a new, more enlightened way.

2

Childhood in the Country

Start with the moment of my birth, June 5, 1923, almost nine decades ago. Much of what I relate about that event must be hearsay, but certain facts are inescapable. Contrary to the initial appearance of most babies who parents and friends find adorable, I must have made a distressing sight. Of course, I don't recall what I looked like exactly at birth but, a few years later, there exists a photo of me on a tricycle. My head, which appears too large for my body carries a set of elephant ears as appendages. I can only surmise what they might have looked like astride an even smaller head. My nose was overly prominent, my jaw protruding belligerently as if I had been born looking for a fight. My eyes were slits and receded deeply in their sockets. My hair, dark and lacking any curl, fell limply as straw across my forehead. At the time of my birth, the nurses had to have been superb actresses to conceal from my family their true reaction to such an unsightly baby.

There were, however, more serious circumstances surrounding my delivery. After bearing four children in her island homeland of Crete, then settling in America, my mother suffered a series of miscarriages. She lost four or five fetuses in the ten years between the birth of my closest brother, Mike, and her pregnancy with me.

During her hours of labor before my birth, the doctors fearing another miscarriage and its possible lethal impact upon my mother's weakened system told my father that to save my mother's life, the birth should be aborted. Their opinion was that mother and baby could not both be saved.

My father pleaded for a little time and went from the hospital to his church a few blocks away to light a candle and to pray. When he returned to the hospital a while later, I had been delivered safely and my mother deemed out of danger, as well.

My father would tell this story in later years as evidence of the power of prayer. Since I have no other explanation, I have no reason to dispute his belief.

I HAVE FEW RECOLLECTIONS of my infant years. I do recall one of my sisters calling out the window to friends in the street below that she couldn't leave the apartment because her baby brother had pneumonia and diphtheria. I learned later that I had those illnesses when I was two.

When I was about six, I remember a tantrum after I was denied something I wished to do and, in my rage, bashing my head against a dining-room buffet. Naka, the devoted Swiss lady who lived with my family for twenty-five years and who looked after my sister and me, scooped me up in her arms and ran carrying me to the corner pharmacy where the pharmacist sought to stem the bleeding. That frenzied flight as I screamed and bled profusely is one of my sharpest childhood memories.

Random impressions, fleeting and fragmented, hang over the next few years. Crying at night to be picked up and cradled by Naka. Quarrels with my sister who had been born a year after me. The smells of my mother's kitchen, the firmness of Naka's hands when she bathed me, the pain of a blow inflicted by a playmate with whom I had fought.

The memories become sharper when I remember the small summer cottage where I spent a number of my greening years.

In the 1970s I wrote and published a memoir titled *Stelmark*. That book's title had its origins with a small rustic cottage my family owned in a rural region in northern Illinois. Our subdivision was called Rabbit Hill and the general area bore the name of Fox Lake, one of the largest lakes in the area. My sister Irene and I spent our summers at the cottage as children under the care of Naka.

The cottage was a rudimentary box-shaped frame dwelling set on wooden posts that were later replaced with concrete posts. It consisted of a single family room separated by plasterboard partitions into a small, closet-sized kitchen, and a pair of cramped bedrooms with space only for a bureau and narrow cot beds. The most engaging part of the cottage was the screen porch that was as large as the rest of the house.

Since the cottage lacked electricity, we used kerosene lamps for light in the evening. Naka did not believe in wasting fuel and, in addition, had an obsessive fear of fire, so the lamps were rarely lit. We went to bed at twilight and rose with the dawn to eat breakfast on the porch, the emerging sun flickering across the mesh of the screens that were coated with dew.

In our final years in the cottage we replaced the kerosene lamps with electricity but we never acquired indoor plumbing. For the decade or so we lived in Fox Lake, our water for washing and drinking came from an old rusty–hinged pump in the yard. Shivering outside in the first frosty mornings of early autumn, thrashing the pump handle vigorously for five minutes before a trickle emerged and then, when the stream grew stronger, splashing ice-cold water across our bodies was a crucible of Spartan endurance.

An outhouse, a shabby frame structure similar to those made infamous in cartoon and story, served our toilet requirements. When sheer necessity forced its use, we shared the malodorous interior with flies, squirrels, beetles and spiders.

As if that simple dwelling were a French chateau or Spanish villa, my older brothers and sisters decreed the cottage should bear a stately name.

My father's full name was Rev. Mark Emmanuel Petrakis. My mother matched it with her own imposing maiden name, Stella Evanthoula Christoulakis. My siblings joined syllables from both my parent's first names and anointed the cottage, STELMARK.

A few days after schools in Chicago closed for the summer, one of my brothers drove Naka, Irene and me to the cottage. On the way we stopped in the town of Fox Lake, about fifteen miles from our cottage, to purchase groceries. When we arrived at the cottage, we opened the doors and windows to banish the musty smells of winter and dusted the spiderwebs from the corners. After Naka made us a light supper, my brother would drive back to the city and we were left on our own for the remainder of the summer.

The biggest change from the inner-city neighborhood in Chicago where we spent most of the year was the silence. This stillness was most noticeable at night as I lay in bed in the darkness. In place of the rumbling of city traffic, I listened to the chirping sounds of cicadas and the occasional lament of an owl. In the morning, we were awakened by the warbling of sparrows and robins. Our breakfast on the screen porch consisted of cereal, milk, toast and jelly. While outside the cottage, dew sparkled on the shrubs and flowers.

After breakfast, we had a boundless terrain of pastures and woods in which to play. Irene and I were joined in our games by the Schroeders, brother and sister, and by the twin boys of the Wilder family. They were neighbors who lived in our subdivision of Rabbit Hill year round.

Betty Schroeder was about my age, a pretty and willowy blonde-haired girl with slender legs, and arms and cheeks browned by the sun. We spent years playing together, but I first really noticed her when we were both about twelve. Perhaps this sharpened perception came about because she had a habit when playing games that required running of tucking the hem of her dress into her cotton panties. That was a vision I found more distracting the older we became.

Betty's brother Robie, who was several years younger, followed us around like a miniature human bloodhound. My memory of him was that he seemed always in need of wiping his dripping nose.

The Wilder twins, Eric and Luther, were also blond and blue-eyed. Since both brothers were about my age, the three of us were zealous competitors in all our games.

From time to time, I'd catch glimpses of the Wilder and Schroeder parents but for the most part my days were spent playing with Betty, Robie, Eric and Luther.

We played a variety of games in the woods and pastures. Hide-and-seek was popular since a cornfield with rows of tall cornstalks and a tree-clustered orchard allowed for numerous places to hide. Another favorite was kick-the-can. We also played a game of war, a small herd of cows in Haisler's cornfield becoming an invading army. We maneuvered stealthily within the cornfield to elude them and, finally, we attacked. Our confrontation with these bovine armies reached a climax when Luther mounted the back of one, digging his heels into its flanks, goading it to charge us. The animal, its head bent, continued chewing placidly on the grass.

My father was the only member of my family who visited the cottage regularly, coming out for a day or two in the middle of the week since his Sundays were devoted to church. On those nights, I knew he would be arriving from the city I would lie restlessly in the darkness doggedly resisting sleep. When I heard the sound of the train whistle passing the railroad crossing in Ingleside, I knew that it wouldn't be long before my father's arrival.

A short while later I saw the headlights from the taxi in the road flash across our cottage windows. With the lights from the taxi enlarging his shadow as he crossed the lawn, my father would enter the cottage. Naka held the screen door open while vigorously brushing away vagrant flies and mosquitoes seeking entry around him. My sister remained asleep but I'd eagerly watch my father unpack the small suitcase he carried. He would bring loaves of bread smelling of yeast and sanctity from his church, glistening apples and oranges, and candy as a special treat for my sister and me.

Afterwards, I'd return to bed while my father retired into the small bedroom separated from us by a curtain to read for a while by the light of a kerosene lamp. I'd hear the crinkling of the newspaper as he turned the pages, and watch the lamplight from below the curtain flicker across the walls and ceiling of my room. Reassured by my father's presence, I'd slip seamlessly into sleep.

MY FATHER WOULD WAKE ME very early in the morning for our day of fishing. In preparation for his arrival, I was required to dig up a hundred worms. That was the number my father requested since he feared a repetition of his dismay when he once found himself anchored in a rampant school of fish and, seeking to bait his hook, discovered he'd run out of worms.

Digging up that quantity of worms was a tedious task. Since my father never used more than fifteen to twenty in any single day's fishing, I gave up digging when I reached that number.

As we walked down to the lake, my father repeated the same question he asked every day.

"Did you dig up a hundred?"

"Yes, Papa," I'd say, averting my face so he would not detect the falsehood.

We reached the pier where several long shiny power craft belonging to more affluent residents of our subdivision were moored. Our seafaring vessel was a small shabby rowboat. I cannot remember if it bore a name. Settling the oars into their sockets, my father rowed us to the center of Fox Lake.

We spent the day fishing while around us a waterscape of serenity flourished. Across the lake, a few fishermen in their boats were visible, casting rods that flashed in the sun. Along the shore, houses reflecting the bright sunlight glowed like tiny bonfires. Around our boat, water lilies sparkled pinpoints of light while butterflies vied with flies for space around our heads.

My father seated in the stern of the boat impassively studied the cork bobbing placidly in the water at the end of his bamboo pole. He didn't seem bothered by hours passing without his hook attracting a nibble.

But through the long monotonous hours of morning and afternoon while we fished, my patience eroded and time dragged for me with agonizing slowness. The only distraction came when we paused to eat the ham and cheese sandwiches and drink the lemonade Naka had prepared for our lunch. Another interruption from the boredom came when I voided into the milk bottle we carried for that purpose.

Sometimes my father caught a small sunfish or perch that he pulled in with the delight of a man snaring a marlin. But even such minuscule catches were rare.

One summer day, my patience finally at an end, I blurted out, "Papa, what do you think of sitting here hour after hour staring at a cork that never moves?"

My father looked at me in surprise, perhaps for the first time recognizing my boredom and impatience. Finally, he spoke in a quiet voice.

"I am thinking how quickly the time is passing, and how soon I will have to leave."

After that day, although I still dug up his supply of worms, he never woke me to go fishing with him again. Several times I heard him at dawn when he rose and thought remorsefully of my transgression. I considered rising to join him, but I never fished with my father again.

In the hunting season, my father was also an avid pursuer of rabbits and birds. I would accompany him on hunting forays through the pastures. I found that pursuit a little more exciting than fishing, even though my task was only beating the bushes to rouse the prey. Even as a boy, I didn't mind my father not allowing me to shoot. To this day I have never felt any redeemable pleasure in a sport that killed living creatures, although I never shared those feelings with my father.

For the most part when my father wasn't there, my days at the cottage were spent in leisure and play. When we weren't playing, I often read. There was a large crabapple tree in the yard back of the cottage, its shade providing an ideal terrain to lie on the ground with a book. Sometimes, swept away by the power of a story I was reading, I'd stare up through the branches at the flickering vestiges of sun. In those moments I thought for the first time of how wonderful it would be if I could someday write stories of my own.

THE COTTAGE AND ITS SURROUNDING TERRAIN were the locale of my initial and then aggressively active onanistic activities. My sexual awakenings had their origins during a two-year period I spent ill in Chicago with a diagnosis of TB, and had been confined to bed. With the thin fabric of my pajamas making masturbation effortless, I began the practice then. As I grew older, during the leisure of my days in the cottage, these masturbatory exercises became more elaborate. I am certain my imagination and excitement were stimulated by the sight of Betty Schroeder's dress tucked into her panties.

In the beginning, I drew on illustrations of underwear models in the Sears Roebuck and Montgomery Ward catalogues. A new paradise of concupiscence opened for me when I discovered the more explicit girlie magazines on the rack in Charlie's gas station/grocery about a half mile from our house at the corner of U.S. Highway 12. When I first opened one of those magazines whose titles I remembered as *Film Fun* and *Fun Fest* innocently sequestered between copies of *Life* and the *Saturday Evening Post*, I was struck by the lightning Adam must have experienced when God sent him the first woman. Unlike the lifeless, one-dimensional mannequins in the department store catalogues, these girls were totally naked, every hilly mound and nested crevice clearly defined. In addition these beauties were always smiling flirtatiously, coyly invoking a salacious response.

Since Charlie, the good and moral owner of the filling station would never have sold me the magazines (even if I could muster the required quarter,) I resorted to stealing them. This was accomplished by my lingering over a coke, tensely awaiting that moment when a car pulling up to one of the gas pumps would summon Charlie outside. Alone in the store I'd move swiftly to my nefarious mission. I'd raise one trouser leg and, using several strong rubber bands, I'd tie the illicit magazine just below my knee, then lower my trouser over it again. I'd resume sipping my coke, until Charlie returned. I'd linger a few more minutes, trying to appear casual despite my heart throbbing wildly. Then I'd begin a slow, tortuous effort at a casual withdrawal, praying that the magazine wouldn't slip loose from the rubber bands and plummet into glaring sight at my ankle before I got out the door.

Later, alone in some isolated corner of the pasture, I'd leaf through the magazine slowly, pausing aghast before each generously endowed blonde and brunette beauty until I selected one to assist me in achieving my fevered release. Meanwhile, in the trees around me, robins and sparrows warbled their shrill tunes of reproach.

Another variation I used to achieve my sodden pleasure was to anoint one of the magazine beauties with a name such as Carmela, Aphrodite, or Rosemary. Using a lined pad frayed and soiled from frequent handling, I'd write a crude story in which I played the part of impassioned lover to one of those beauties.

"I heard Carmela's oven-hot voice calling from the bedroom. When I walked in, she was stark naked, her breasts pointing at me like daggers! 'My lover!' she cried. 'Take me! I'm yours!'"

Whether utilizing magazine photos or stories I'd written, those were idyllic interludes I spent in the deserted pasture. If some wanderer had stumbled upon the scene, he would have seen a gangly youth sprawled on the grass, trousers and underwear tugged down to his knees, oblivious to anything but the pages of *Film Fun* and *Fun Fest*. He might also be intently reading the barely legible, ink-smudged scrawls of his own lurid stories with one hand clutching the paper while the other hand vigorously whipped that hapless organ that distinguishes the male from the female body.

In all the letters and journals I have read of other writers through the years, the famous and the obscure, I cannot recall any of them recording that they first began writing their stories to supplement the rituals of masturbation.

DURING ONE OF OUR LAST SUMMERS at the cottage, a girl of about nineteen, named Christina (I cannot recall her last name) came from Chicago to visit one of our neighbors. She brought with her the searing beauty of reality in contrast to my puerile paper fantasies. She was small in stature, slender, and stunningly lovely with soft golden hair that cascaded across her shoulders. Although she was five to six years older than the rest of us, Christina joined our games with a child's zest. When our motley group ran across the pasture, she ran with us, her dress swirling about her bare legs and slim bare feet. From time to time I was granted a beguiling glimpse of her silk panties, a sight I found more erotic than any of the photographs of fully naked girls in the magazines.

One day when we were both seated in a rowboat, she in the stern while I sat in the bow rowing, for the hour we circled the lake, my eyes were drawn as if by magnets to the divine recess visible between her parted legs.

During the days that Christina played with us, I never opened one of the magazines. I enjoyed all the sensual delight I needed basking in her glowing presence. More than 65 years later I used the cottage and that lovely girl as the background for a story titled "Christina's Summer."

If Christina were still alive she'd be a very old woman now, never having known what an impression that brief visit she made to Fox Lake had on one of the barefoot youths with whom she played.

My father's visits were always brief, no more than a day or two. At the end of his stay, he departed by taxi, retracing the same route he traveled when he arrived. On those days he returned to the city, my sister and I rode in the taxi with him into the town of Fox Lake. He'd buy us a soda and a comic book in the general store. Then we'd wait with him in the depot until the great bell-clanging and steaming black locomotive pulling a coal car and several passenger cars entered the station. He'd kiss us a final time and then board his train. He seated himself at one of the windows facing the station and waved to us through the glass. We waved back as the train pulled slowly and sonorously from the station. Afterwards the taxi transported us back to the cottage.

THE COTTAGE EVOKED FOR ME many happy, carefree memories but there were unhappy memories, as well, one of them comprising the most agonizing summer of my childhood.

My beloved Naka who looked after my sister and I with diligence and devotion would once or twice a year go on an alcoholic binge. I had no idea how her drinking started but it may have been the reason her husband drove her from their home in St. Louis and brought her and her son, Alex, to come and live with us.

Because I knew her so well and loved her so much, I could tell at once when she had been drinking although my younger sister seemed unaware of these changes. But I noticed quickly how the liquor brought a glow to Naka's eyes and a slight slurring to her speech. When these episodes of her drinking occurred, they produced an intense anxiety in me and I waited tensely for the two- or three-day ordeal to end.

For some reason unknown to me to this day, one summer, Naka began drinking in June soon after we arrived at the cottage and didn't stop until the day in September when we returned to Chicago.

I'm not sure how Naka covered the cost of the cases of beer I saw being delivered. She had no income beyond the few dollars my father gave her each week. I suspect the charges for the beer were probably concealed in the grocery bills my father paid.

Naka would begin drinking before my sister and I rose in the morning and continue drinking all day. Most of the time she was able to function except for those few occasions when I remember her so sorely affected by the drinking that she became disabled, sprawled across her bed and snoring in the middle of the day. When my sister noticed that something was wrong, I told her that Naka wasn't feeling well.

Naka's drinking also produced eccentric behavior. She'd forget she had prepared lunch and, in early afternoon after we'd already eaten, make us a second sandwich. At bedtime, she'd bring us each a glass of milk and then, ten minutes later bring a second glass. Sometimes I'd refuse the milk but most of the time I drank it to spare her any distress.

Drinking also produced irrational fears in Naka. When Farmer Haisler's cows broke free from their pasture and milled about our cottage, in a fit of terror Naka frantically pulled down the shades and crouched with us in a corner of the room.

When a storm arose, lightning and thunder battering the cluster of trees around the cottage, she'd summon Irene and me into her bed. The three of us huddled together clutching a crucifix while Naka prayed fervently for our salvation.

I suffered with Naka all that summer, unable to understand what compulsion was keeping her drinking day after day. I remember one night when my sister and I, sleeping in cots on the screened porch, which we did when the weather was excessively hot, were wakened by a heavy storm driving rain through the screens. Naka came from inside the cottage to lead us to our beds inside. Her voice was focused and sharp, as it was when she was sober and I hoped feverishly that night might mark the end of her drinking.

Several hours later, when daylight woke me, with a despairing heart I saw Naka had begun drinking again.

There is another memory of the cottage linked to my father when one day two neighbors brought my father a petition protesting the entry of the first Jewish family into our subdivision.

"We've got nothing against Jews, Father," one neighbor said. "But they should live with their own kind. Once one of them moves in, then all the rest will follow."

As a respected Christian priest, the neighbors said, my father's signature would carry substance on the petition.

I sat in a shadowed corner of the porch, out of the beam of the kerosene lamp, and waited for my father's response.

My father told our neighbors he'd be pleased to add his name to the petition. As our delighted neighbors unfolded the petition before him, my father told them of one requirement before he could sign. His boss would have to sign first.

"You mean you need your bishop's signature first, Father?" one neighbor asked.

"No, no," my father said gravely. "My big boss, Jesus Christ. If he signs, I'll be happy to sign."

WE SPENT SUMMERS IN THE COTTAGE until I was about fourteen and my sister a year younger. By that time, we missed our friends in the city and my father's duties at the church made his visits less frequent. At some point we simply ceased making our summer excursions to Fox Lake.

The cottage stood empty for a few years after my father's death in 1951 when we sold it for $5000, $500 down and the rest payable by note over a five-year period.

Although I do not remember their names, I have not forgotten the husband and wife who bought the cottage. They were an older couple, the husband nearing retirement, both of them excited as newlyweds about acquiring that modest refuge from the turmoil of the city.

Within a year, however, the wife died of cancer and the husband, stricken with the same disease, died a few months later. I do not know who inherited the cottage after their death.

Once, some fifty years after our summer sojourns in the cottage, on assignment from a Chicago paper to revisit that location of my childhood, my wife and I drove from Chicago to Fox Lake. The cornfield adjoining our cottage which once held Haisler's cows and long rows of corn had been developed into an upscale subdivision of perhaps a hundred homes, each with its own garage and manicured lawn.

The cottage, STELMARK, much smaller and shabbier than the garages and tool sheds belonging to the adjoining houses was still standing but was being used as a storage shed by another resident. The outhouse and pump were both gone.

I also visited the cottages where the Schroeder and Wilder families lived, but ownership of those homes had changed numerous times through the years and the residents I spoke to, knew nothing about those families from my childhood.

Down the road at the lake, at the water's edge, the pier had been enlarged and improved. Half a dozen powerboats and several sailing craft were anchored. There wasn't a trace of the dilapidated rowboat that ferried my father and me in pursuit of those flourishing pockets of fish he was sure swarmed tantalizingly just out of reach.

Along U.S. 12, at the gas station, Charlie had retired but still lived in the same house next door to the station. We spent a convivial afternoon with Charlie and his wife Ann, and their daughters, revisiting those childhood experiences. I confessed to Charlie then about stealing his magazines. He told me he knew about my theft but with an uncommon generosity of spirit decided not to expose me to my father.

In looking back upon that period of my childhood, what I could not comprehend as a boy and only came to understand after many years was the importance of that simple cottage to my father. For my sister and myself, Fox Lake meant several months of play unrestricted by city fences or traffic. My father came to the cottage seeking a refuge from the tribulation and grief he endured in his parish.

His church duties included counseling scores of parishioners on emotional problems in their lives. Whether he could help or not, the endless litany of confessions must have burdened his spirit and weighed on his body. Although I could not understand the reasons, I saw the consequences of those emotional grievances he had to endure in the way he seemed honeycombed with weariness each evening he returned home from church. I'd bring him his slippers and he'd offer me his blessing. Afterwards he leaned back against the headrest and wearily closed his eyes.

I had to become an adult before I understood the anticipation with which he rode the train from Chicago, and his melancholy and regret when the time came for him to ride the train back to the city.

To this day almost seventy-five years after those summers we spent in the cottage, hearing a train whistle at night carries me back to those nights in Fox Lake when I fought sleep, awaiting the taxi that would bring my father from the train.

3

Childhood in the City

I wrote earlier about my illness causing us to miss two summer vacations at the cottage. The disorder began when I was about twelve. Unlike other boys my age possessing boundless energy, for a few months I felt a growing listlessness. My apathy roused the concern of my parents, and Naka took me to our family doctor. A series of x-rays revealed tubercular lesions on my lungs. The only therapy in those days (except for those families who could afford a sanitarium in the mountains) was bed rest. Our doctor ordered me to bed for a month.

I came home excitedly from that first visit to the doctor to undress and jump into bed while it was still daylight. Since I felt no different than I had before the cheerless diagnosis, my initial reaction was elation. I was being spared doing homework that evening and, as an added bonus, I wouldn't have to go to school the next day. Even more reason for joy, I would experience that vacation bounty for a whole month!

I'm not sure how long that euphoria lasted but after a month when we visited the doctor again, and he prescribed a second month and following that a third and fourth month of bed rest, the elation passed. I entered a period when my days were filled only with boredom and despair.

My confinement to bed came before the advent of television. There was radio, but the programs I found exciting (*Jack Armstrong, The Shadow, Lights Out*) weren't broadcast until evening.

I began by reading comic books and adventure stories in the pulp magazines, which I quickly exhausted. As my confinement continued, I turned to more substantial books, at first drawing on our home library. When those books had been read and I asked for more, my brothers and sisters started bringing home books they'd purchased from the sidewalk stalls of bookstores for 10 cents to 25 cents apiece. There were novels and travel books, histories and memoirs. I was especially drawn to the classic adventure novels which I read and re-read, *Captain Blood and Scaramouche* by Rafael Sabatini, *The Count of Monte Cristo* by Alexander Dumas. I also loved nature stories such as *White Fang* and *The Call of the Wild* by Jack London. About that time I read Jack London's novel *Martin Eden*, the story of an unlettered seaman who taught himself to write became one of the most influential books in my life.

When I read that novel the first time I enjoyed it, but did not grasp its significance until a second reading some years later. By that time I had dropped out of school in my high school sophomore year. Suddenly, that moving story of the young, self-educated sailor dreaming of becoming a writer became my dream.

Through the course of several months, perusing one weighty tome after another, I read the complete *Book of Knowledge*. For those weeks I burrowed into those volumes, my dreams teemed with random events and dates, snatches of history and lines of poetry. I think the reading became a refuge for me, a sanctuary against a growing depression bred by inactivity.

After almost a year in bed, my condition worsened. A cough developed in my chest and with it a nagging pain when I took a deep breath. The handkerchief I held to my mouth became speckled with blood. I was weary of bed, suddenly scared of what was going to happen to me. My room had become my prison.

Our family doctor began visiting me to spare my traveling to his office. One evening after he had examined me, I heard him speaking in a low voice to my parents. I rose from my bed to crouch in the doorway of my room and heard him telling my parents gravely that my condition had become critical, and that I needed to be sent to a sanitarium. I did not know what sanitarium meant but I equated it with a dying-place from which I would never return.

My parents and Naka sought to reassure me, but I was convinced I would be sent away to die. In terror of being transported to the dying place while I was asleep, each night I desperately fought to remain awake. Night after night, Naka sat with me in a chair beside my bed until exhaustion closed my eyes.

There were events during that period of illness that remain vivid for me to this day. The first was the entry into my life of two girls, perhaps 17 to 19 years of age. Both came from city orphanages to live with us, their principal duty to help care for me. My mother provided them room and board and gave them some spending money each week. One girl was named Olga and the other girl Mary. I cannot remember their last names.

Olga came first. She was a stocky, robust Russian-Orthodox girl who limped because one leg was several inches shorter than the other. She also had a large discolored birthmark blemishing one side of her throat. She had a habit of rubbing her fingers roughly against the stain, as if trying to wipe the blemish away.

Olga was a powerful girl whose strength, at first, frightened and then fascinated me. When she changed the linen on my bed, I'd sit in the armchair and marvel at how easily she lifted and flipped the mattress. I was also intrigued by her strong, unsightly hands with stubby broken nails that she chewed down to her fingertips.

From time to time Olga would light a cigarette that she smoked near an open window, brushing vigorously with her hand to disperse the smoke.

"You don't say nothing to your father or mother now, you hear?"

I'd nod that I understood.

"If you do talk, you know what I'll do to you?"

I'd nod again feeling an excited tightness and fear in my chest.

She'd chuckle and wink, raising one of her broad, strong hands,

"You'll get this," she said slowly, relishing the effect she was having on me, "You'll get it you know where . . ."

"I know," I'd say.

Olga bullied and teased me, never with cruelty but in a playful demonstration of her dominance. She'd lift me easily from the bed in her powerful arms and I'd see the glaring birthmark on her throat and the small hairy moles on her cheeks. On one occasion when she was putting me back in bed she gave me a light teasing smack on the seat of my thin pajama trousers.

I was fascinated by Olga, encouraged her disapproval, relishing her mastery and control over me. She began threatening me with spankings if I "wasn't a good boy." With a mixture of excitement and fear, I went out of my way to disobey her. She obliged by spanking me, first on my pajamas, and, finally, on my bare buttocks.

The firm but playful spankings seemed to fulfill a strain of dominance in her and also nourished a strain of submissiveness in me. They also evoked erotic feelings in me I had never experienced in the same way before.

Then, one morning at the beginning of autumn, Olga was gone, replaced by Mary, a plump sweet-faced girl who smelled of lavender. There was nothing strong or assertive about Mary who was feminine and soft and evoked different feelings in me than those I'd felt with Olga.

I can still recall the soft sheen of Mary's skin, her breasts and nipples embedded against her blouse, and the tantalizing glimpses I caught of her slender legs and thighs when she bent to make my bed.

We became more intimate with one another. When my mother was on her daily charity rounds and Naka out of the house shopping, Mary and I in the apartment alone, she'd recline on my bed beside me. Feeling her close and inhaling her scents, I couldn't resist reaching out timidly to touch her. In the beginning she slapped my hand away but after a while her resistance softened. She allowed me to caress her hair, cheek and ears, my fingers moving warily down to her throat.

"Do you think I'm pretty?" she asked.

"Yes . . ."

"Do you think I have nice skin?"

"Yes . . ."

"Do you like my eyes?"

"Yes . . ."

"Do you like my . . . ." She left the word unfinished, but one of her fingers fluttered across her breast.

"Yes . . ." I said. "Oh yes."

Slowly I became more daring and I reached for more intimate parts of her body. When she didn't object, excitement and desire made me even bolder. A marvelous moment came when she allowed me to touch her naked breasts. She also guided me gently into the first kisses I had ever known.

Slowly, over a period of weeks, my intimacy with Mary became more brazen. In the beginning she stripped to her slip. After a while she peeled off that garment, as well. Wearing only cotton panties, she snuggled under the sheets beside me.

She talked to me sweetly, her eyes closed, as if she might be imagining someone older and more mature lying beside her. She stroked my chest and arms, encouraging me to caress her. I had seen my sisters in brassieres but Mary's breasts were the first I had ever seen naked and I marveled at their symmetry and their resilience, the way her nipples sprang back after my touch. One cataclysmic day, perhaps excited by my caresses, she slipped her hand down beneath the sheet and touched my genitals. Despite her touch being light as a bird's wing, it generated a wild surge of heat through my body.

Then Mary was gone, as well, replaced by a prune-faced old woman appropriately named Barboonis, who came in to help Naka with the housework and look after me. The old lady was sexless and humorless, smelling of sweat and garlic, making my room appear dark and dismal no matter whether it was morning or night. With each passing day, I mourned anew the loss of Olga and Mary.

To this day I understand the influence those two girls had upon my life. By awakening in me those early surges of sensuality, they left in me fetishes of playful spanking and illicit caresses that remain tantalizing to this day.

ANOTHER EVENT FROM THAT PERIOD of my illness that stands out came one Christmas, an ebullient holiday in our large family. My brothers and sisters allowed me to sprawl on the living room couch and watch while they decorated the big pine Christmas tree they had carried in earlier. The room was permeated with the fragrant smells of fresh pine as my siblings began placing lights and ornaments on the tree.

"Those lights are too close together. They're lopsided!" Barbara, one of my sisters, would say.

"Your head is lopsided!" my brother Mike replied.

"Put the silver ornament higher!" my sister Tasula said.

"Stop shaking the ladder!" my brother Dan cried.

One of my sisters made sweet, steaming cocoa, gilded with snowy whipped cream floating on top. As I sipped the cocoa, my brothers and sisters transformed the bare-branched tree into a majestic pillar of lights, ornaments and tinsel, the peak adorned by a sparkling star.

During the second Christmas of my illness, after the tree had been decorated, my brothers carried into the room a large bulky carton they placed alongside the tree.

"What is that?" I asked.

"None of your business."

"Who is it for?"

"It's for you. But you won't get it if you don't go to sleep."

Despite my heated protests, I was sent back to my bed in the adjoining sun-parlor room. But the knowledge that the large carton contained some mysterious gift for me kept me sleepless. I felt myself on the verge of some miraculous revelation. Finally, weariness overwhelming my excitement, I fell asleep.

On Christmas morning Naka woke me and led me into the living room where my parents, siblings, and Naka's son Alex, all in pajamas and robes, were crowded into the room.

My brothers had completed their work after I had fallen asleep for around the base of the tree was the mysterious gift that had been in the carton, a gleaming electric train on a circular silver track—a black, sleek locomotive, a chunky coal car, and a string of bright yellow passenger coaches, the cutouts of miniature figures framed in the tiny windows.

My family enjoying my delight, I was given the transformer to hold on my knees. I moved the switch carefully. The marvelous train responded, circling the track slowly at first, gathering speed as I pushed the switch higher. Finally, whistling like the wind, the train raced round and round the track, the coaches lurching, the wheels spinning furiously, sparks flaring from the silver rails.

I learned later that the train had been the main prize raffled off at the *Avalon,* the neighborhood theater where my sister, Tasula, worked as a cashier and my brother Mike served as an usher. The winner, unmarried and childless, offered to sell the train for ten dollars.

My brother (after a hasty phone consultation with my father) made the deal and brought the train home. So on a raffle won by a childless man, the magnificent electric train became my treasured possession.

I played with the train through the holidays, running it round and round the glistening tree. I made tunnels from boxes and created forests by lining the track with my mother's plants. At the beginning of January when the tinsel, ornaments and lights were taken down and the pine tree hauled away, the train was moved into my bedroom and connected around the foot of my bed, the transformer placed beside my pillow.

During the months that followed, the train filled the lonely recesses of my hours. I sent it on its journeys in the light of breaking day, the rays of pale winter sun filtering weakly through the windows. I drove it in the twilight, the beam of the locomotive flashing through the shadows, lights gleaming in the tiny windows of the coaches.

In my fantasies I became the engineer of that Cannonball Express, roaring across the limitless expanse of the country, speeding through valleys bordered by mountains, racing by small, sleeping towns, crossing bridges suspended over massive canyons. Riding the winged, swift fury of the train, controlling its power by the barest movement of my fingers I was provided the means to flee the fear of my illness and the stifling prison of my room.

Long after I had recovered from my illness, during the Christmas holidays, I would sometimes unpack the train and set up its tracks and cars. The task grew more difficult as time passed because the tracks had grown bent, the locomotive light did not work, and the coal car had a broken axle. All these impediments made me finally pack the train away for good.

I forgot about the train for a number of years until one day—after I was married and had left my father's house—cleaning out the storeroom in the basement of a building from which my parents were about to move, I found the locomotive of my train, a shabby and battered relic. There wasn't a trace of the coal car, passenger coaches, or any of the sections of track. Holding the locomotive in my hands, I remembered the wild, jubilant journeys we had shared. I was tempted to keep the engine but because there seemed something childish about remaining attached to a childhood toy, I threw the old relic away.

THERE WERE OTHER TREASURED MEMORIES of childhood after I had recovered from my illness and was able once again to join my friends. Among the games we played in our alley playgrounds, was kick-the-can, that sport where a goalkeeper guards the can. Once a player is spotted, the goalkeeper taps the can with his foot and calls the player's name. The player is then consigned to jail and only the successful kicking of the can by another player will free him.

Our games of kick-the-can were expansive, sometimes numbering up to twenty-five or thirty players. Among all the games of kick-the-can we played in the alleys of summer, one stands out for me in a heroic dimension.

The goalkeeper had managed to capture all the players but two, my friend Marvin and myself. When Marvin was captured, I became the only player still able to rescue my twenty-five jailed companions. From my hiding place in one of the yards I could hear their imploring voices, "Harry, save us . . . you're our last chance . . . Harryyyyyyy!"

I crept stealthily from yard to yard, crouched behind a row of garbage cans, and then shinnied up a telephone pole to the roof of the garage directly above the jailed players in the alley. As I waited tensely on the roof, the nervous goalkeeper stared to the right and to the left, never imagining that the attack on the can might come from above.

With the entreaties and pleas of my companions echoing in my ears, I watched warily as the goalkeeper wandered further and further from the can. When I felt he had gone too far to make it back before I attacked, I leaped from the roof to an adjoining telephone pole and slipped swiftly to the ground. The shrieks of my companions alerted the goalkeeper who came racing back . . . but not before I had given the can a furious kick that sent it rolling and ricocheting down the alley. My companions joined in a thunderous ovation as they scattered. The goalkeeper stood stricken for an instant and then collapsed in tears on the stone of the alley.

Some cynical reader might observe that however I seek to ornament the memory, the whole episode was no more than a childhood game of kick-the-can. But if it were only a game of kick-the-can, why do I recall the experience so gloriously after seventy-five years? It was for me a gilded moment of unmatched triumph and jubilation I have been vainly trying to match in my life ever since.

IN THE MID-1930S, our small movie theater located near Vernon Avenue and 61st Street in our Washington Park neighborhood was called the AMO. The structure had a shabby facade and a dingy marquee with a display always missing letters so that the title "Scarface" became "Sc rfa e." There were more elegant cinemas on the South Side including the TOWER, the TIVOLI and the AVALON but the AMO was the cheapest and the one closest to where I lived.

I cannot remember the shop that adjoined the AMO to the west but to the east, close as the pouch of a baby kangaroo to its mother, was a candy store. This shop was so narrow and cramped a compound that it barely held enough space for a glass candy counter and an antiquated popcorn machine that groaned as it spit out the kernels. The window of the shop held a small bowl of assorted hard candies and a Coca-Cola placard featuring a beguiling blonde beauty with a tooth-powered smile.

The shop was owned by Mr. Bilder, a slightly built, pale-cheeked Greek immigrant with a sad, nervous smile. What I recall most clearly was his gentleness and patience. With only a couple of pennies to spend on candy, selecting from the racks of caramels, mints and chocolates was a crucial decision—one delayed as long as possible. Yet through the lengthy ponderings by my companions and myself, I can never recall Mr. Bilder exhibiting a trace of impatience.

After purchasing our candy, we'd hurry to the movie box-office. The Saturday matinee doors opened at one o'clock with the movie starting at two, but a crowd of us would be waiting in line, well before one. When the doors were opened, we surged into the lobby, clutching our tickets. The ticket takers were often old men, tufts of hair sprouting from their gaunt chins and out of their withered ears. Despite their warnings that we walk, not run, we raced to claim our seats, changing places several times, before settling on a location.

The afternoon show started with one of the serials that ran week after week. There was *The Phantom Empire, Perils of Nyoka* and *Zorro's Fighting Legion*. Another of my favorites was *Flash Gordon* played by the muscular, dynamic Larry "Buster" Crabbe, who each week fought valorously to keep lovely Dale Arden from the menacing clutches of Ming the Merciless.

Saturday after Saturday, I marveled at how Flash managed to escape Ming's destructive death ray or avoid burning to death in a conflagration that Ming ignited. All through these serials, bells tolled, clocks ticked, wheels whirled—all devices used to heighten suspense. They served their purpose as we vigorously booed the villains and loudly cheered the heroes.

After the serial segments came the feature films. There were any number of them I cherished, among them *Frankenstein, The Bride of Frankenstein,* and *Mutiny on the Bounty.* A comedy I especially enjoyed was *A Night at the Opera* with the Marx Brothers, in which the crafty business manager played by Groucho Marx, turned the tables on various snobbish characters seeking to thwart him. As the film finished we'd leap from our seats to rush up and down the aisle mimicking Groucho's crouching walk.

During one summer of matinees, a real-life drama vied with the films for our attention. A pair of merciless invaders from the North Side of the city bought the AMO and installed their own candy counter in the lobby.

We were outraged and vowed our loyalty to Mr. Bilder. We not only continued to buy our popcorn and candy from him, a small group of us even pledged to boycott the AMO hoping to bring the callous new owners to their knees. But the theater had signs sternly forbidding any outside popcorn or candy. Our bags of popcorn from Mr. Bilder were confiscated while we had to carry the bars of candy deep in our trouser pockets, to be retrieved and eaten furtively in the dark theater. Several boys with oversized bars that ushers and the manager spotted, were exposed and evicted.

Our plans for a boycott of the theater were also foiled. As Saturday neared and another exciting serial with Flash Gordon loomed, our resolve weakened, our outrage not strong enough to make us relinquish the joy of those matinees. We slipped quickly by the candy store to buy our tickets. Ashamed to face Mr. Bilder, we avoided patronizing his business and hastened his demise. One Saturday matinee, I noticed the front door of the candy store was locked, the shade drawn on the door.

OUR DISDAIN FOR THE THEATER OWNERS did not prevent some of us from working for them distributing handbills of coming attractions. Our pay was a free admission to the Saturday matinee.

About a dozen of us would assemble in the lobby early in the morning while one of the managers would distribute the handbills to us along with a stern warning that the most heinous crime we could commit was to dump undelivered handbills in some alley trashcan.

To discourage this practice, older boys were appointed to monitor us. We had several names for them, one of the less onerous being "Rats." As we made our rounds, slipping the little leaflets into doorways, mailboxes and under windshield wipers on cars, the relentless "Rats" followed in our wake.

Recalling those years, there were many feature films that sparkled like gems through my adolescence—*Little Caesar, I Am a Fugitive from a Chain Gang* and *King Kong.*

The film that had the greatest impact on me, which I first saw when I was 14 or 15 was *All Quiet on the Western Front,* the story of young German schoolboys in the First World War who join the army in a patriotic fervor only to experience despair and disillusionment in the brutal years of warfare that followed.

Those schoolboys despite being German, were close enough to my own age, so I suffered with them the terrifying days and nights of incessant shelling, the senseless charges across No Man's Land to capture a patch of land they would lose the next day, the wounding and suffering of comrades.

Forty years later while I was writing *The Hour of the Bell,* my novel on the battles of the Greek Revolution against the Ottoman Empire in 1821, I drew on the emotions I'd felt while viewing *All Quiet on the Western Front.*

Meanwhile, as Saturday matinee after Saturday matinee came and passed, alongside the theater, the small store of Mr. Bilder receded further and further into the shadows. The Coca-Cola beauty in the poster faded, the glass bowl of candy gathered dust, the plate glass window darkened. After a while, hurrying to those Saturday matinees I loved so much, I hardly noticed the candy store at all.

4

Education

My elementary school education began at Koraes, the Greek-American parochial school attached to my father's church on Chicago's South Side. Although the school became fully accredited later, at the time I attended, classes only went to the sixth grade and Koraes wasn't able to graduate students. After finishing the sixth grade, students moved on to A. O. Sexton, the neighborhood public school, for two additional years before graduation.

The starkest difference between our school and the city's public schools were the beatings administered at Koraes. The English teachers struck us as a matter of contractual obligation, but the Greek teachers, true to their passionate Mediterranean background, beat us with dedication and fervor. To this day I find it hard to remember what subjects I was taught at Koraes, but vivid memories of the beatings remain.

Although I had enjoyed Olga's playful spankings during my childhood illness, I took no pleasure in the relentless rods and rulers of our teachers as I frantically tried to avoid these beatings upon my palms or across my legs. Regardless of the stoicism we endeavored to display before our classmates, a few blows across the legs would send us into what we called the "Koraes Syrtos." (The Syrtos being a popular Greek folk dance.)

Among all the teachers I remember from the years I spent at Koraes, none of them stands out with the brutal clarity of a principal we had for a two-year period. I will not reveal his real name in consideration for any descendants who might feel aggrieved at this maligning of their deceased relative. I will give him the name we used to describe him then—"Mr. Beast." In Greek, the phonetic sounds much harsher; his name would be "O Ke-re-os Ag-re-os."

If not in demeanor, certainly by his conduct he was indeed a beast, a gorgon lurking in the corridors waiting to pounce upon some hapless miscreant. For some unfathomable reason (perhaps to demonstrate that despite my father being the parish priest, I could still be punished) he seemed to have developed an affinity for me and I suffered the cursed stick for the most trivial of infractions.

My main order of business as I attended school each day was to avoid Mr. Beast as if he were the plague. That was easier hoped for than accomplished. One morning, trying to slip unobserved past the open door of his office, he spotted me and barked my name.

I entered the office trembling and he rose from behind the desk to greet me, the stick in his hand. (We swore he slept with the bloody weapon.) He came toward me, his face so close to mine I smelled the garlic on his breath.

"What evil have you done today?" he hissed.

Now it was still early in the morning and I had scant time to commit any mischief. Secure in my innocence I shook my head fervently and said, "Nothing! Nothing!"

Mr. Beast's response was to bring the stick down hard across my right calf. Quick as an agile athlete he raised the stick and struck my left calf. I began to dance the "Koraes Syrtos."

When I could finally focus my pain-blurred eyes and adjust to the thunder in my ears, it was only to see the malevolent countenance of Mr. Beast intoning, "That is for the evil you will do tomorrow!"

MR. BEAST WAS ALSO OUR TEACHER in Greek history and religion. A good portion of his religion classes were spent in describing Hell, where he assured us, we were all destined to end up one day. He'd describe the searing of those eternal flames with such meticulous authenticity that we swore he must have visited the place as a tourist many times. To this day, I can remember his blazing denunciation.

"Pet-rak-ees!" he'd single me out, his voice hoarse with wrath. "You are going to Hell! And there you'll find all your wretched and worthless friends waiting for you!"

His analysis of Greek history was also fundamental. Our ancestors were philosophers, warriors, poets and dramatists. We were maggots destined to live puerile, useless lives. He was so fervent in his denunciations that we couldn't help believing what he was telling us was true.

I remember once making an effort to surpass the lowly expectations of Mr. Beast. That crucible came on a day when I was in the fifth or sixth grade and had forgotten the small brown bag with my lunch at home.

When noon came, our teacher walking up and down the rows of desks, noticing I had nothing to eat, asked about my missing lunch.

I cannot account for the flight of fantasy that possessed me then. Instead of a simple, truthful explanation for the reason I had no lunch, my imagination took flight like a gull. I told the teacher that on my way to school that morning I had passed an old beggar sitting in the street. Swept by feelings of compassion, I had given the old beggar my lunch.

As that simple lie sprang buoyantly from my tongue, I was unprepared for the reaction from my teacher. She stared at me with an expression of delight and wonder. Then she called one of my fellow students to fetch Mr. Beast.

For a panicked moment I feared she had perceived my deception and that the monster was being summoned to punish me. When the student returned with Mr. Beast (carrying his ubiquitous stick) my teacher called the class to attention.

"We have all enjoyed Harry reading his make-believe stories to us," she said. "Today he has a true experience to share. I want you all to listen carefully and let this marvelous act of Christian love and charity become a model for conduct in your own lives."

She turned to me, her voice softening.

"Harry, please repeat that marvelous story again."

I had told a quick, simple lie to explain my missing lunch. But with the entire class hanging on my words, with the menacing Mr. Beast standing there, and in the very first row a lovely dark-haired beauty named Penelope watching me . . . Penelope was the loveliest girl in all the school and I and every other boy in my class adored her. That young beauty had never given the slightest indication she knew I was alive. Now, lovely Penelope was watching me, listening, waiting.

In such circumstances, I could not repeat a simple little lie. I had to make it a Homeric proclamation! So on the spot I began to ornament the fictional encounter. I spoke of the old man's ragged clothing looking as if it had been washed and mended many times, the way his fingers trembled with weakness from hunger when he took the bag of lunch from my hands, the tears of gratitude that glistened in his eyes. Finally, I replicated his trembling voice when he thanked me by saying, "God bless you, my boy."

When I finished my recital, for the first time Mr. Beast touched me without the stick, tapping my shoulder in approbation and pronouncing me, "a good Christian boy." My classmates were so awed they neglected to applaud. Penelope, the exquisite Penelope was so profoundly moved that she could not hold back tears in her lovely eyes.

Walking with my head bent in a demeanor of seemly modesty, I returned to my desk, which I found stacked with portions of the lunches of my classmates. There were halves of cheese, bologna, and ham sandwiches, vanilla wafers, Oreo cookies, Fig Newtons and slices of cake. There were apples, oranges and bananas, enough to stock a fruit market. And yes, from Penelope who rose from her seat and with the grace of a Homeric princess, walked to my seat in the rear row and with her slender, delicate fingers laid upon my desk like a votive offering, one golden, juice-swollen peach!

That fleeting moment of triumph gleams like a starry constellation to this day. Basking in the admiration of my classmates, I took a bite from a bologna sandwich, responding to a student on my right.

"Harry, Harry, how did you think to do such a thing?"

"I don't know," I said. "Something just came over me, I guess."

From a student on my left, "Harry, you know you'll be number one in the school from now on!"

"I know . . ." I murmured. "I know."

At the pinnacle of my deceptive glory, the door of my classroom opened and my mother entered.

She was my mother and I loved her. For an unthinking moment, I was glad to see her and raised my hand in an affectionate wave. It wasn't until my teacher walked to greet her and I saw the small brown bag my mother carried in her hand that I had the first intimation of the catastrophe that was about to befall me.

To this day, I cannot remember just what took place then, what my mother said, what the teacher said, what Mr. Beast did. After all, when we are young, tongue-lashings and beatings bounce off our sturdy frames.

One thing I do remember from that day, and will remember for as long as I draw breath on this earth, is how Penelope left her seat in the first row and with the grace of a Homeric princess walked to my desk in the rear row. And how, with her slender, delicate fingers, she reached down to my desk and took back her peach!

There are also grimmer memories of those years I spent attending Koraes, one that involved our bitter warfare with the young blacks.

Our neighborhood was a polyglot of immigrants, some fleeing oppression and others seeking the fulfillment of the American Dream. These included Greeks and Italians from Southern Europe, Armenians from the Caucasus, and Jews fleeing Germany where the Nazis had taken power.

There was also a domestic migration. During those Depression years, Chicago was also receiving a large black population from the Jim Crow South. As their need for housing space increased, black families moved east and south in the city, entering the environs of our neighborhood. The white population began to move east toward the lake. After a few years, our parish school and church became a block-long oasis in an all-black neighborhood. We felt ourselves a community under siege.

Directly across 61st Street from our school, was a Catholic church and parish school in which, reflecting the neighborhood, the students were black. Our religious affiliation as Christians did not temper our hostility toward the color of their skin, which, in the primitive tribal assessments we measured by then, marked them as mortal enemies.

Our two schools were separated by 61st Street, and by iron fences that enclosed our schoolyards, but those barriers did not prevent daily confrontations, when we shouted epithets and hurled stones across the street from one schoolyard to the other.

Outside those fenced enclaves, when we met singly or in small groups, we battled savagely, most often with fists but at other times using bats and sticks, causing injuries and often drawing blood.

The fiercest battles of our year came at Halloween, when we formed gangs of as many as 50 black and white youths and prowled the alleys in search of our adversaries. When we met in a darkness broken only by faint streamers of light falling from kitchen windows, a wild confrontation erupted, a shrouded conflict of punches and kicks.

Afterwards, washing and tending wounds that might easily have been inflicted upon us by one of our own, we felt the pride of battle-hardened warriors, boasting of the destruction we had wreaked on our adversaries.

Over the years, I have often wondered with remorse and bewilderment as to what impelled us to such enmity then, and why we hated and feared the young blacks so much. I cannot say my feelings reflected those of my parents, because I never heard my father or mother condemn anyone for the color of their skin. They had also been victims of discrimination when they first emigrated from Crete to the United States so that my father might serve a community of young Cretan coal miners in Price, Utah. Because of their dark complexions, the Cretans were also thought to be of African origin and were subjected to the same prejudice. The Cretans proved unruly and resentful and in armed confrontations fought back with pistols and rifles against state militia and the mine owner's police.

But I had been born after my family left Utah, and had no experience of that discrimination and struggle. All I felt as a youth was that the skin color of the young blacks marked them as dangerously different. In addition they were intruders in our neighborhood, displacing us, forcing us to move. Any idea that we might live peaceably side by side, seemed as remote as a trip to Mars.

The older boys in our groups were generally the most effective fighters, and each side had its champion. Ours was a lean athletic youth named George Dionisotis, the swiftest and strongest among us. He was the principal guardian of the caravan of students that walked east together from the school to the safety of our own neighborhood.

When we had George guarding our caravan, we felt more secure. When he led us in battle, we fought with greater confidence and courage.

The champion of the black youths was someone whose name I am not sure about to this day. The closest I can remember was hearing someone call to him in a fight using a name that sounded like "Shelby" but it might have been another name.

He was about 14 or 15 at the time, graced with height and strength beyond his years. Once when a dozen of us, evenly split between black and white were fighting, I caught a glimpse of Shelby about half a block away and was astonished at how swiftly he crossed the distance between us. Shelby attacked us with such devastating fury, that we were driven into panicked flight.

In addition to his physical strength, there was an aura about him, a dominance we felt overpowering. That invincibility was confirmed for me on another occasion when, feeling ourselves secure behind the safety of our iron fence, our schoolyard teeming with students, we taunted a group of young blacks walking along 61st Street. One of the youths left the others and, as he came racing toward our school, I recognized Shelby. In a single leap he vaulted over the iron fence into our schoolyard. Gripped by a collective hysteria, the entire schoolyard of students took flight for the sanctuary of our school building. The spectacle of that solitary youth chasing 100 descendants of the valorous Greeks at Thermopylae remains vivid with me to this day.

In solemn, chagrined conversation with a few boys afterward, attempting to rationalize our frenzied flight, I referred to Shelby as "a black Achilles." That ignored the fact that Achilles had been a Greek warrior, but the power Shelby evoked and the fear he produced in us cast him somehow in a mythic dimension, and Achilles seemed an appropriate name.

Those shameful, primeval battles continued for as long as I attended the parochial school. One final incident that stands out for me occurred on a morning when I was hurrying to school. Because I was late I cut through an alley and ran squarely into Shelby. I was at his mercy and braced myself for a beating. For an instant neither of us moved and when Shelby hesitated, I realized he wasn't going to attack me. Perhaps recognizing how unequal we were as antagonists, Shelby did not deem me worthy of a beating. But as he turned away, he uttered one word, "Someday . . ." I turned and fled.

To this day, more than 75 years later, I haven't any idea what that word meant or how Shelby might have finished the sentence. Perhaps he spoke it as a warning for some future encounter, or perhaps he meant something else. I will never really know.

Long torturous decades of race struggles have transpired in this country since my adolescence, the Supreme Court's landmark decision in 1954, the defiant lady Rosa Parks, refusing to sit in the back of the Montgomery, Alabama bus, the "Freedom Riders" in 1961 and James Meredith, becoming the first black student to enroll at the University of Mississippi the following year, the Rev. Martin Luther King, Jr., arrested and jailed in Birmingham where he wrote his profound and moving "Letter from a Birmingham Jail" reminding the Christian clergymen to whom the letter was addressed of the words of Jesus, "Love your enemies. Bless them that curse you, do good to them that hate you and pray for them which despitefully use you and persecute you." Then on to the terrible day in 1967 in Memphis, when the Rev. Martin Luther King was assassinated.

If I am certain about anything, I am sure Shelby would have been active in those civil rights struggles, a leader as he had been a leader in his youth.

To this point in time, having achieved the milestone election of an African American, Barack Obama, as president of the United States, beyond the cheering crowds, the unfurled banners, the pride and hope of not only African Americans but those of other minority races and nationalities in this country, I see the imposing shadow of Shelby and remember as well the solitary word he spoke then: "Someday . . ."

If the black Achilles of my youth is still alive, he would be an old man now as I am an old man, and he, too, might be remembering those brutal encounters of our youth while recognizing how time and the long struggle for civil rights have completed the sentence he left unfinished.

Perhaps Shelby might also accept this moment in our nation's maturing as a kind of redemption and atonement for those barbaric and senseless battles we fought against each other in our youth.

I DID MANAGE TO FINISH the six years of Koraes and then spent the following two years attending the A. O. Sexton Elementary School. I have a tenuous memory of graduating and, the following fall, beginning as a freshman at Englewood High School on Chicago's Southwest Side.

I completed my first year at Englewood and began my tenure as a sophomore. The classes I most remember from this period were in R.O.T.C., the Reserve Officer Training Corps for which I showed a marked affinity. The grizzled veteran army sergeant who directed the program called me "a born soldier" because of my grasp of field combat fundamentals. He told me he had never before awarded any freshman cadet a promotion until his sophomore year, and then gave me my corporal's stripes that first year as a bounty for my performance. I am sorry to admit that I did not prove worthy of his expectations.

My sophomore year in high school began with problems. The two years I had spent in bed reading had provided me a vocabulary and knowledge of literature far beyond that of the average high school sophomore. Of course, my fellow students were far ahead of me in science and mathematics. I also lacked any of the social graces and found difficulty assimilating to my fellow students. I started playing truant and, finally, ceased attending school at all.

About this time, beginning to recognize with mounting concern my abhorrence of school, my father decided to send me to the University of Illinois in Urbana Illinois where my brother Mike was attending school.

My brother was living in a rooming house occupied by a group of young Greek students who had banded together to form a rag tail fraternity called Epsilon Epsilon Epsilon. They provided a room for me in their house and I enrolled in an Urbana high school.

But the habit of truancy I had practiced in Chicago returned.

I'd leave in the morning from the rooming house, but instead of attending my high school class, I'd find one of the numerous libraries that existed on campus. I'd locate a secluded corner and settle into one of the armchairs with a book.

After a while my brother became alerted to my truancies and began tracking me down. Soon after I left the house in the morning, he'd set

Chapter 4

out on his ritual of pursuit. He would check one library after another until he found me.

When I looked up from the book I was reading and saw him, neither of us would say a word. I'd close the book and put it back on the shelf. Then I followed my brother to his small coupe. Once inside the car, we'd sit for a few moments in silence. Finally, my brother spoke.

"I don't know what I'm going to do with you," his voice registered dismay and resignation. "If you keep this up, what am I going to tell Dad?"

I had no answer and after a few more minutes of pained silence, my brother would start the car and we'd drive off.

In more remorseful moments, I promised my brother I'd cease my truancies. For a few days, I'd attend my classes at school. Then, as if attendance was aberrant conduct I couldn't control, my truancies would begin again.

My brother kept warning me that he'd tell my father, but he never followed through on his threat. That is, until another episode of my misconduct.

The year was 1939 and war had begun in Europe. The American Student Union was a group that among other issues was resolved to dissuade Americans from entering the conflict.

I was conscripted into the organization by an older boy, lean-cheeked and intense, I remember only by the name of "Gooze." He epitomized irrevocable logic as he explained the reasons our country should avoid becoming embroiled in the European conflict.

Even though a number of years had passed since I'd seen *All Quiet on the Western Front,* that picture's strong antiwar theme still resonated with me and helped condition my favorable response to Gooze.

At the end of our conversation he clasped my hand tightly and told me in a fervent voice:

"We need fellows like you . . ." I felt a surge of pride in being one of those fellows.

I began attending the American Student Union meetings, admiring the eloquence with which the speakers made their case.

Since I was a new and a very junior member of the organization, my task was the rudimentary one of passing out leaflets denouncing intervention in the European War.

For the most part, our meetings were uneventful until one large assembly was disrupted by another group of students, accusing us of being unpatriotic because we rejected our country joining those allies in Europe battling the monster Adolf Hitler.

Fighting broke out between the two factions, and although I do not remember any personal confrontation in which I defended our cause, a general melee wasn't resolved until a half dozen police squad cars with wailing sirens and flashing lights appeared.

The riot ended when perhaps a hundred of us were hustled into paddy wagons and driven to the local police station. We were not booked, but were sequestered in a bullpen until parents or other relatives came to claim us.

From within the cell, I saw my brother appear, his expression more anguished than when he found me in one of the libraries.

When we were in his car, he clutched the wheel in both his hands and spoke in a desperate voice.

"How am I going to explain this to Dad? What am I going to tell him? You tell me what I'm going to tell him?"

I felt remorseful for causing him grief, but I had no plausible answer.

My brother finally felt he had to tell my father what had transpired. My distressed father, at his wit's end, resettled me from Urbana, Illinois to a Catholic parochial school named St. Procopius in Lisle, Illinois. He felt the stricter environment prevailing at that institution run by the Jesuits, where troublesome youths were sent for disciplining, would benefit me.

MY TENURE AT ST. PROCOPIUS lasted all of two weeks. Every other class seemed to involve religion and all classes were conducted by vigorous young priests in their somber black cassocks. They were passionate, stern and avidly eager to give some impertinent boy a sound smack across the ear.

When they joined us at baseball, the young priests rolled up their cassocks and tied them around their waists. They were our coaches and they were fiercely competitive and not averse to using curses to censure or inspire a player.

"Larry, you son-of-a-bitch, get the lead out of your dead ass and cover your base!"

"Morgan, another botched play like that and I'll cut off your balls!"

I don't have any plethora of memories from my brief stay at St. Procopius. One episode I do remember came at the end of my first week in a class on religion taught by a sturdy and athletic young Jesuit named Father John. (The school had a dozen priests with that name.)

In Fr. John's religion class, he pronounced the rite of baptism an essential requirement for salvation. Those not baptized were doomed to the blazing fires of Hell. In the question period afterwards, I raised my hand and, when called upon, I asked whether that would be true in the case of a newborn baby dying a few hours after birth without any chance at baptism.

Fr. John's response was brief and emphatic.

"If it wasn't baptized the poor, unfortunate child would be consigned to hell."

I protested that harsh conclusion hardly seemed compatible with a just and benevolent God. Fr. John insisted there wasn't any discrepancy. After a few moments, seeing him growing irritated and impatient at my questioning, I ceased any argument.

But the incident and my question had stirred baleful emotions. Later that day, I was informed by one of the students that . . . "Zarkov wanted to see me under the trees."

I had been at the school long enough to know that "under the trees" designated a grove about a mile from the school where battles and disputes between the boys were resolved. I also had a sudden uneasy recall of Zarkov as an oversized Russian Orthodox convert to Catholicism. There was a certain brutish quality about him that suggested one should avoid provoking him.

"What does he want with me?"

"I dunno nothing," the boy said. "I'm just giving you the message."

"What if I don't go?"

"That would make Zarkov madder."

Spurred by a frail hope not to make Zarkov any madder than he already was, I started apprehensively toward the grove of trees. When I approached, I saw a cluster of a dozen St. Procopius boys. Looming above any of the others, much more of a behemoth than I remembered him from previous sightings, was Zarkov.

When he saw me, Zarkov lumbered toward me. He wagged an enormous finger menacingly in my face.

"You make fun of God," he said in a harsh, accusatory voice.

"Me?" I said, genuinely perplexed. "I didn't make fun of God! I would never do that! I respect God!"

Zarkov shook his head, rejecting my protests.

"You make fun of God," he said with a finality that suggested further explanations were useless.

"My father is a priest!" I made a final plea. " Believe me, I love God!"

He shook his head rejecting my appeals. He raised his fists, which loomed in front of him like a pair of large hams and motioned me closer. I was at once bewildered at why my simple question to Fr. John should have provoked him, and also terrified of the beating the monster might inflict on me. For a moment, I considered taking flight, racing back to the protection of the school buildings, and then realized that I could not continue to evade Zarkov if he were determined to fight.

I advanced haplessly toward the oversized Russian, raising my fists while trying to hide the tremors that racked my body. We moved slowly toward one another. When we came within arms length, Zarkov suddenly lashed out with one of his feet (bigger than his ham-like hands) the toe of his hard leather shoe ramming into my crotch. The pain was ferocious and I plummeted to the ground, clutching that rudely assaulted portion of my anatomy.

My final memory of that confrontation was Zarkov bending over my agonized, writhing form, once again wagging a huge hand in my face.

"You no more make fun of God!" Zarkov said.

A few days later the rector of St. Procopius, (another Father John) called me into his office.

"We've notified your father, Harry, to arrange to come and get you. We don't feel that you and our school make a good mix. Good luck elsewhere."

FOLLOWING MY BRIEF SOJOURN at St. Procopius, I offered my parents what seemed to me a plausible course of action. I planned to leapfrog from my sophomore year in high school directly into the University of

Chicago. I convinced them I could do it and perpetuated this charade by visiting the registrar at the University of Chicago, a gracious lady named Miss Valerie Wickham, and making an impassioned, eloquent case for my being allowed to take entrance examinations. Apparently, I made a convincing argument because the sympathetic lady granted me permission to take entrance exams the following spring for the school year beginning in the autumn.

I began studying for the exams, but after a period of time lost interest. I had discovered the allure of gambling, and when the time came for me to take the exams, I never showed up. However, I informed my parents I had passed the tests. Brothers, parents and friends congratulated me, none of them bothering to investigate and confirm my fraudulent claims.

In the end, the six years at Koraes, two years at A. O. Sexton elementary school, a year and a half at Englewood High School on Chicago's South Side and two weeks at St. Procopius comprised the totality of my formal education.

To mention here that I am now also the holder of half a dozen honorary degrees is not to suggest that my erratic journey was justified.

Lest any young aspiring writer use my meager academic resume to justify their own indolence and downgrade the value of education, let me warn them that the course of my life has been a bewildering series of incongruous events. There is no lesson to be learned besides the obvious one that an outcome often depends on the vagaries of chance.

In the end, abandoning my formal education did not impede my life as a writer. At the same time, if I had remained in school, perhaps some perceptive high school or college teacher might have recognized in me some glimmering of writing talent and been able to offer me guidance. Under more enlightened tutelage, I might not have had to serve a ten-year apprenticeship before selling my first story.

5

Addiction

My obsession with gambling began when I was sixteen and lasted until I was twenty-four—two years into my marriage. I cannot be sure when I stumbled from pastime into addiction. In the neighborhoods of my youth, friends and I played hearts, pinochle and nickel-ante poker. One day Red, two years older than I was and my closest friend, took me for the first time to the local handbook, a shabby, cavernous room in an abandoned warehouse. I was repelled by the smells, sights and sounds of that malodorous room and the sallow, haunted faces of its inhabitants. Yet, after a while that shabby enclave became my home away from home.

For the next few years, I spent endless hours in that dismal room among a flock of dreamers, pigeons of the scratch-sheet tip and sparrows of the fifty-cents-across-the board parlay. There were times I felt it embracing me like a womb and, later, when I wore the addiction like a second skin, searing me as if I were in an anteroom of Hell.

As a race at one of the half a dozen tracks running across the country began, men and women clutching their tickets swept in a wave to stand beneath the loudspeaker as if the circular web of metal and wires were some mesmerizing deity. The finish of a race was met by a few cries of jubilation. More often there were muttered curses or a forlorn shaking of heads. People stared at the winners like ghosts at a feast.

Red, who had been wagering on horses for years, led me through the mystical labyrinth of gambling. He taught me to study the bloodlines of horses and the rudiments of betting—the variations between win, place and show. While my parents thought I was attending school, Red and I were intently reviewing the day's entries in the racing form we had studied diligently for hours the night before.

There were entire days I spent locked within that womb of dreamers, experiencing the turmoil of losing and wining. The races at various tracks went off in rapid succession, leaving scant time for speculation or regret. As one race finished, we rushed to the window minutes before another race at a different track was called. I spent the day experiencing fleeting moments of euphoria when I won and dejection when I lost.

I never thought of Red or myself as addicted. We were simply players, small-time sports trying to beat the odds in a profession as old as prostitution.

The truth was that we were addicted and no longer in control of our lives. That was proven for me on a day when I left Red my tickets for a half dozen parlays I had bet, linking horses so if one steed won, a larger sum would be riding on the others.

After making my bets, my habit was to retreat to the neighborhood library to read for a few hours and then, late in the day, return to the handbook to check my wagers.

That afternoon, when I returned to the handbook, four of the five horses I had parlayed had won. With my eyesight blurring and my heartbeat racing, I confirmed the winners several times. When I left the handbook I had figured my winnings totaled almost $500, in those days of fifty cent and one-dollar bets, a fortune.

Red and I worked part time in a neighborhood liquor store and as I hurried to work I considered giving Red 10 percent for shepherding my bets and cashing my tickets. Deciding that was overly generous, I determined 5 percent would be a more judicious figure, as well as to set a precedent for future winnings. As I was to discover soon enough, Red had already chosen his percentage.

In the liquor store, Red was serving a customer and as soon as he finished, he motioned me to follow him into the store's back room crammed with crates of wine and beer.

"Can you believe it?" I cried. "Four winners out of five! Unbelievable! The biggest score of my life!"

His despairing face rejecting my jubilation, Red somberly removed his glasses.

"Hit me," he said in a despondent voice. "Hit me."

I felt the first inkling of calamity.

"Hit me," Red pleaded. "Hit me."

Finally, tears in his eyes, his voice trembling, he confessed that celebrating my good fortune he had cashed in my tickets. He figured that luck was running our way, and that I wouldn't mind his borrowing a few dollars of my winnings to make a bet of his own. When his horse lost that race, he borrowed still a few more dollars from my winnings. When he had lost a hundred dollars, he became frantic at having to explain the loss to me and he kept betting, whirling feverishly from one track and one horse to another in a desperate effort to regain the money. In the end, he lost every dollar of my winnings.

I was heartbroken and barely listened to his tearful promise to split his weekly salary with me until the debt was repaid. To this day I cannot recall whether Red ever made a payment or how much of the debt he eventually repaid.

The highlight of our gambling year came in the summers when the Chicago tracks were open. Half a dozen young sports would join Red and me to travel on the Illinois Central train south to Washington Park. Our journey among equally cheerful passengers was raucous and buoyant, our motley group exuding the euphoria of drunks who had not yet had a drop of liquor, but who were heady with anticipation. When we emerged from the train, the beaming sun and the excited crowds streaming alongside us toward the entrance to the track, added sparkle to our ebullience.

Seated high in our grandstand seats, we alternated a chorus of cheers and groans as the races began and ended. Between races, we intently studied the racing form.

"Gila Water is a cinch in the 5th!"

"The nag is even money!"

"A winner is a winner!"

"Favorites are for chumps!"

What each of us yearned for was to have a winning ticket on a horse no one else had bet.

At the end of the day we walked back to the train strangely content, despite the money we had lost. The sheer thrill of wagering and then watching the pageantry of the races trumped all other emotions.

Days such as that were the high point during those years, the camaraderie, the excitement, the enduring of numerous defeats in exchange for that triumphant moment when one of our horses crossed the finish line in first place.

But there were many low points, as well. Pawning my brother's suits, selling my sister's books, stealing from the register of the store where I worked, all to nourish the gambling that had become the obsessive focus of my life

I understood I was on a slippery slope to destruction and I tried a number of times to quit. But without the excitement of the gambling, my days seemed sterile and desolate. In order to make my meager funds last as long as possible, I also tried to ration my gambling. One week, having won $100, I resolved to play no more than $10 a day, so the money would last me ten days. As a precaution on the first day, when I departed for the handbook, I left $90 at home under my mattress.

After I lost the ten dollars, I went home and retrieved another $10. When that was gone, I walked home for another $10. Even when I understood that before the day was over I was going to gamble the full $100, I continued to make the futile eight block walk back and forth from the handbook to our apartment, my anger and futility at my losses and at my weakness growing more virulent with each trip. By the end of the afternoon, the $100 lost, I was left not only broke, but also exhausted and enraged.

I THINK THE FIRST STEP toward my deliverance began on one of the most desolate days of my life. That occurred several years after my marriage, my wife pregnant with our first son. Along with a partner I had bought and was operating a small lunchroom. (More about that devil's anteroom later.) The first of the month had arrived, and I lacked money to pay rent on the lunchroom as well as the gas and electric bills on our studio apartment in Kenwood.

Not for the first time, I went to my father, who however limited his own resources, never refused me help. I left his church office that day with $200 in cash, the full monthly salary he received from his parish. With a few dollars of my own in my pocket, on my way back to the lunchroom, I stopped in the handbook to make what I promised myself would be a single bet. When the horse lost in a photo finish, frustrated at how close I had come to victory, I dipped into the $200, taking $10 to bet another horse. When I lost the ten dollars, I was faced with the ordeal of having to explain to Diana the reduced amount. I bet desperately, again and again, until, late in the afternoon, when the last races at the various tracks had been run, I had lost my father's $200.

In total despair, I returned to the lunchroom, which Diana had closed. In the shadowed interior lit only by a dim overhead lamp, I found my wife sitting at one of the tables, her cheeks stained with tears. She was also frightened at what might have happened to me. Having to undergo the humiliation of confessing to her what I had done, for the first time I recognized the malignancy of my transgression and the depth of my addiction.

I don't think I stopped gambling immediately after that night, but the experience marked the beginning of my healing and over the next few months I gambled less and less and finally stopped. The sheer immensity of my betrayal of my father's generosity and the pain I had caused my wife made me aware that if I did not salvage my life, I would become one of the lost souls I had seen in the handbook—burned-out men and women without allegiance to anything or anyone except those interludes of excitement as the races were run.

At this point in time, reviewing the landscape of my life which along with its sorrows, the death of loved ones and the illness of friends, has also provided me peaks of fulfillment with my marriage, the birth of our sons, the publication of my books, travels to my parents' homeland of Crete and the treasure of friendships.

None of this bounty would have been possible if I had not survived the gambling addiction that could have destroyed my life, as it destroyed the lives of so many others.

Yet, for as long as I live, I will never forget the gilded euphoria of those festive mornings when Red and I with our rag tail group in tow, rode the train to Washington Park. In those sun-bright beginnings every conceivable triumph was still possible, every extravagant dream able to be fulfilled. And as another stately caravan of horses paraded slowly and majestically to the gate for the beginning of a race, we had still one more chance to achieve redemption and glory.

6

Courtship

I have this memory of first seeing Diana Perparos, the girl who would become my wife, in the second or third grade of our church parochial school. In my recollection, she appeared skinny and a little awkward. What I recalled most vividly were her large, sparkling and intense dark eyes.

A period of years passed from that time until we met again in our teens. One Sunday while attending church, I saw Diana again and I was astonished at how the girl I remembered had bloomed. She was about my age—sixteen or seventeen then, with a flawless complexion adorned by her great black eyes. Those were unchanged. What was different was the disappearance of any skinniness or awkwardness, her figure filled out into an alluring slenderness. Her raven-black hair was also longer, tumbling from her temples across her shoulders.

The season must have been summer because she wore a light print dress, high heels and a broad brimmed straw hat that framed her lovely face.

The only faint marring of her beauty were the braces she wore on her upper teeth, braces not evident unless she laughed. As if she were conscious of them, when she did smile or laugh, her hand fluttered to her face in a self-conscious effort at concealment.

I cannot remember the words we exchanged at that initial meeting. Since we both lived in neighborhoods east of the church, she in Hyde Park and I in Woodlawn, we rode the trolley east together. She ascended the trolley steps before me, her dress hiking up well above her knees. I was treated to the sight of her slender, shapely legs in silk stockings and, pressing against the light shimmering fabric of her dress, the contours of her stunning buttocks.

In a story written many years later, I described one of my female character's buttocks as "contrapuntal" beauties. I first thought of the word that Sunday with Diana. I confess that to this day I'm not sure whether the word can sustain any coherent application to the female anatomy, but the true meaning of the word is less important than the mellifluent way it captures my first impression.

We began to date, sharing casual evenings at the Reader's Drug Store on 60th Street near the Midway and the University of Chicago, where we lingered over cherry cokes. We also patronized Fluky's on 63rd Street to while away the time while eating their savory hot dogs. In between dates, we conducted lengthy phone conversations, lasting 45 minutes to an hour. For the life of me, I cannot recall what we spoke about during those calls. Since I had five siblings in my family, each one with their own social calendar to be fulfilled, I was heatedly berated for "hogging the phone!"

Diana had graduated from Hyde Park High school and had moved on to study secretarial skills at McCormack College in Chicago. She would have wished to have gone to a regular liberal arts college to continue her education, but her father, John Perparos, had his shoe repair/cleaners totally destroyed in a fire, with the loss of all his stored clothing and racks of shoes. His insurance agent assured him that he would be well within his rights to repay his customers a small percentage of their claims, but John Perparos insisted on repaying what his customers told him were the full cost of their lost garments.

"These good and loyal people brought me their business!" he said fervently. "They trusted me! I won't let them down now by cheating them on the price of their clothing!"

The result of his effort to be fair was that after all the claims were satisfied, his business hung at the edge of bankruptcy.

Diana's older sister Maria, who was as lovely as Diana and had more than one suitor, was working as a manager in an upscale restaurant on South Shore Drive.

Feeling her family's financial needs required precedence over her own desire to attend school, Diana found work as a hostess/cashier at a restaurant in South Shore called the Wilshire.

To my dismay, when she entered the workplace she also came to the attention of other men who found her as lovely as I did. I was outraged when she confided to me the disgraceful attempt of the restaurant bookkeeper, a married man in his sixties, to steal a kiss! While that lout was easily repulsed, for the first time in our two-year relationship, I found myself confronted by rival suitors.

I had grown bigger and older since I first saw Diana. I don't think it boastful to say I had a pleasant temperament and a good sense of humor. However, I felt these weren't enough to compensate for the lamentable disparity in my features. Because I was forced to look at myself in the mirror each morning and evening, I was daily reminded of my shortcomings. At the time, I still had a head of bushy dark hair. Below the hair my eyes were small and deep-set, my nose oversized with a hawkish curve, my lips thin. The most disappointing part of my anatomy remained my large and unshapely ears, one a half inch longer than the other, giving my head a lopsided appearance. In addition, both ears had lobes so large they might have provided another pair of ears for a more conventional head. I found scant consolation in that Abraham Lincoln and Buddha had similarly oversized ears. When I compared my appearance to that of Diana's loveliness, we seemed an incongruous couple.

I would travel to the Wilshire restaurant in the late afternoon, waiting for Diana to finish work so we might ride the bus or IC train home together. On one of those visits, I met her principal admirer whose first name I cannot remember, but whose last name was Thorman. The marauder was taller than I was by at least two inches, blond-haired, flawless-eared, with a smile Diana described as 'nice' but which I was positive had a serpentine allure.

Desperate to find a playing field on which I could compete, I drew upon the fertility of my imagination to keep Diana entranced. I described ordinary daily experiences to her with dramatic flourishes. A visit to a grocery became an odyssey in which I ran into various colorful characters. My tales about them produced the desired appreciation and laughter from Diana.

When enhancing my experiences were insufficient, I invented imaginary encounters with friends and neighborhood characters. I also shared with her my excitement about books I had read. I gave her *Martin Eden* by Jack London and *The Gates of Aulis* by Gladys Schmitt, two books that had an enormous influence on me.

I CONFESS NOW to an even more lurid example of my creativity. Having admired the flashing swordplay in adventure films starring Tyrone Power and Robert Taylor, I had begun taking fencing lessons at Hermanson's Fencing Academy in Woodlawn. I began sharing with Diana stories of the people I met and fenced with at the academy. The year was 1940, Europe was engaged in a war that most Americans were anticipating the United States would join. One of the fencing students at the academy was a youth of German extraction whose first name was Helmut. I had a minor altercation with him, and in relating the experience to Diana I added a few frills. Her genuine concern that I might get into more serious trouble with Helmut nourished my propensity to storytelling.

Anxious to provoke further evidence of her solicitude towards me, I invented more serious disputes occurring between Helmut and me. He had shoved me in the locker room and I shoved him back. We had fenced in a duel against one another and after a heated, violent contest, settled on a draw.

I found myself trapped in my own exaggerated storytelling. In order to heighten the drama, I had to keep inventing more and more colorful details. One night, in desperation to keep the suspense mounting, I told Diana that Helmut and I had a violent confrontation. We resolved to fight a duel with our foils stripped of their rubber tips. That lethal confrontation meant that I might incur a mortal injury.

The effect upon Diana was all I could have hoped. I told her the duel was set for the following evening at midnight after the Academy had closed and the fencing academy was deserted. With tears in her eyes, she pleaded with me to refuse to fight the quarrelsome German. I kept insisting that, for honor's sake, the duel had to be fought.

The evening preceding the contest we spent together, Diana was tearful and solicitous, and more loving than she had ever been. I basked in the glow of her concern and, as we parted that night, I pledged I'd phone her first thing in the morning.

Before retiring that night, I walked in front of the closed fencing academy, seeking to absorb some of its ambiance as I contrived a way to resolve the imaginary duel. The outcome I preferred was to claim I had slain the villainous Helmut. But that would have required explaining how I had disposed of the body. Nor was I certain whether or not Diana would wish to continue dating a killer. I decided on a less lurid outcome.

I slept fitfully that night and rose at dawn to use our family bathroom before my siblings rose. With the bandage and tape I had purchased, I affixed a sizeable piece of gauze to my chest. I stained the edge of the bandage with a little iodine to represent blood.

When I phoned Diana, her apprehensive voice answered almost at once. She told me she hadn't slept all night. Even as I felt a twinge of remorse at my fabrication, I told her that an exhausted Helmut had conceded defeat. But in achieving my victory, I had sustained a minor wound.

Diana insisted I come see her at once. I traveled to Hyde Park and to her apartment where she greeted me at the door. She insisted on seeing the wound and I removed my shirt to show her the bloodstained bandage. The moment was a glorious one in which I basked in the warmth of her solicitude and her tears.

SEVERAL YEARS EARLIER, not long after we had first begun dating, I had tried to kiss Diana. With what seemed genuine regret she stopped me, saying she feared her braces would be an obstruction.

I had no way of knowing whether that would prove true or not but for the following few years while we dated, fearful of embarrassing her if the braces proved an obstacle, I made no effort to kiss her again. We did hold hands, sometimes shyly caressing one another's fingers.

Then at the beginning of our fourth year of dating, soon after the episode of the duel, sitting on a bench under the shadow of the Museum of Science and Industry one summer evening, our faces close together, we kissed. The sweetness of that long-delayed kiss deserves a poem and not a mere sentence. When the kiss ended, we stared at one

Chapter 6

another with the delight of children who had discovered unimpeded access to a jar of cookies.

Beginning that night and each time after that we were together, we petted fervently, going beyond kisses to caresses, my hands freely poaching under her skirt. Both of us were apparently eager to make up for the years of intimacy we had missed.

That added intimacy brought us still closer together, into a kind of physical and emotional bonding that we accepted would someday bind us in marriage.

In the meantime, with the outbreak of war in Europe, and the relentless advance of the Nazis across France, my feelings about war had changed. The emotional influence on me of the book and film, *All Quiet on the Western Front* with its condemnation of any war had been replaced by a fear and revulsion of Hitler and his Nazi armies. These emotions were further sharpened when the armies of Italy invaded Greece. Instead of swiftly defeating that small country, the fascists were driven back into the Albanian mountains. Winston Churchill, the prime minister of England, said of the valorous Greeks, "We no longer will say Greeks fight like heroes, but rather that heroes fight like Greeks."

For a while my Greek heritage gained me a certain enhanced persona in the environs of our neighborhood.

By early 1942, following the attack at Pearl Harbor, and America's entrance into the war, newspapers printed stories of the fall of France and of the valiant struggle the English people were waging against the Nazis. London was being bombed and our English-speaking allies huddled every night in bomb shelters. My own view of the war matched the evolving mood of the country. All these events spurred my patriotism and sharpened my desire to play my part in that epic struggle.

In my own South Side neighborhood, one of my closest friends, Jack Murray, had just been drafted into service. Two other friends had just been discharged because of war-incurred injuries, Hance Taylor from the Army and Chuck LaMotte from the Marine Corps. Chuck had been among the Marines who landed on the island of Tarawa, and his recounting of that bloody landing and the fighting that followed spurred my outrage and admiration for our soldiers. I was ready and eager to join and do my part as my buddies had done. When my classification became 1A, I awaited my induction into service with enthusiasm.

All the war films so popular then, with their star-crossed lovers playing out their human dramas against the backdrop of world conflict seethed in my head and heart. My evenings with Diana were shadowed by the prospect of my eventual departure to play my part in the great conflict. I confess I played the part of the warrior soon to be separated from his beloved with high and poignant drama.

That day came during the summer of 1943, when I received a notice to appear for my induction into the military. In those final days we spent together, Diana and I shared a series of emotional rehearsals for our ultimate separation. She was solicitous and loving, each of our nightly farewells tender and tearful. Her other admirer Thorman, despite the splendor of his naval uniform, had been banished backstage while I occupied the proscenium of the theater.

Diana's small but fierce-spirited mother, from the beginning of our relationship justifiably suspicious of me as a suitable suitor for her daughter, even appeared to relent. Once or twice as she bade me goodbye, I noticed a tear in the indomitable little woman's eye.

My only knowledge of war had come through books. I was most fascinated by ancient battles, which pitted warriors against one another in single combat. I had read and reread the *Iliad*, swept up by the spectacle of ships sailing to battle on storm-tossed seas. After the landing, the onslaught of mighty armies, the heroism of champions clashing in single combat. Some part of me must have known that none of these reveries had anything to do with modern warfare, but my romantic temperament fused them into a pageant of heroics.

The night before my induction, Diana and I walked in the balmy summer night. By this time we had spoken all the words of farewell and love we could muster. We spent our time together in pensive silence, each of us poignantly understanding that we had become those star-crossed lovers destined to be separated by war. Our final farewell in the stairwell outside her apartment was lingering and tender. Even as I felt some apprehension at what the war might bring for us, I could not help savoring the tears that stained her lovely face. I envisioned myself as Robert Taylor or Tyrone Power bidding his beloved farewell.

The following morning my family and I engaged in a series of endearing farewells. Naka, my mother and my sisters all wept. One of my brothers, Manuel, was already in service while my oldest brother Dan had been granted a work deferment. My younger sister, Irene, was flying in the Civil Air Patrol. My mother had two gold stars in our apartment window and that morning added a third star for her youngest son. Finally, my father gave me communion and all our family shared a prayer. I left the apartment building warmed by their love and their tears.

I joined a group of about a hundred youths my age at a local American Legion hall for a breakfast hosted by veterans of an earlier war. We listened with frequent bursts of applause as several speakers expressed the gratitude our country felt toward us for our valorous response in its time of need.

Following breakfast, we were transported by busses to the induction center where we began a series of medical tests, every part of our bodies probed and measured, screened and assessed. While I wasn't a great athlete I had held my own in running and wrestling contests. A regimen of weightlifting had also enlarged and strengthened my muscles. In looking around at the other inductees, I was grateful to appear to be among the strongest.

The screening process moved at a steady pace, until at the end of a long day, we lined up for final approval. I reached the desk staffed by a corporal who took a draftee's medical papers and motioned him right or left. When I reached the desk I greeted the soldier with a broad smile intimating we would soon be comrades. He stamped my papers and handed them back. I looked down and saw a large and glaring "Rejected-4F" at the top of the first page.

I was stunned! My second reaction was that there had to have been some error in the processing, some misstep on the part of one of the many doctors and technicians who had examined us. I returned to the desk with my query. The corporal referred me to another office where I met a grizzled Army sergeant who reexamined my papers.

To this day I don't accurately recall any precise diagnosis for my rejection. The sergeant himself had no explanation except that in some way, it related to one of the examining doctors finding scar tissue on my lungs lingering from my childhood tuberculosis.

I made my plea to the sergeant, assuring him that for years I hadn't any problem with strenuous exercise. My legs and arms were strong, my breathing good. He seemed sympathetic to my appeal

"You really want to get into the Army?" he asked gravely.

"Yes, yes I do!" I said earnestly, and then, with blustering bravado added, "But not into a desk job! I want to serve in a combat unit!"

The sergeant led me down a corridor to the office of a lieutenant who, the sergeant told me, had the authority to countermand the rejected classification.

The WAC at the desk told us the lieutenant was at lunch but was due back shortly. The sergeant and I sat and waited. From time to time, the sergeant looked at his watch. After about a half hour, the WAC apologized, telling us the lieutenant was usually very prompt in returning from lunch, but that day, for some reason, he was late.

The sergeant told me he had to return to his duties and couldn't wait any longer. He suggested I call back in a few days and he'd see whether he could arrange for me to see the lieutenant.

I LEFT THE INDUCTION CENTER that day still struggling to accept the trauma of rejection. I delayed returning home until later in the evening, struggling for a way to tell my parents and siblings, my neighborhood friends, all honorable veterans of the war, that I had been rejected. Above all, remembering our poignant farewells, star-crossed lovers facing a hazardous future with fortitude, I was mortally ashamed of having to carry that message of rejection to Diana.

When I finally went home, I bought some time with still another lie that I had been asked to return to the induction center in about a week for some special assignment.

I never returned to the induction center to find the sergeant and to try to see the lieutenant. I feared my chances of being reclassified were slim and I would have to undergo being rejected and humiliated a second time.

For the following few days, I struggled with a potential course of action. By the end of the week, born of my desperation, I devised the most expansive lie I had ever concocted.

I informed my family and Diana that I had been chosen to be among a select group studying at a special school for the Diplomatic

Chapter 6

Service. Our ultimate assignment would be to serve in the occupied countries after the war ended. Because of my knowledge of Greek, my probable assignment, I told my family, would be to my parents' homeland of Greece. Needless to say, my family was not only impressed but also pleased that I'd have the chance for the first time to visit Greece.

What aided me in this deception was the secrecy that wartime required. Whenever I was asked a question I had difficulty answering, I was able to invoke, "I can't say anything. You know . . . security." I informed everyone that I had been sworn to secrecy, not even able to tell my family where I would be taking my training.

For several weeks I struggled to formulate my plans, which everyone was waiting anxiously to hear. My family, my friends and Diana asked the question every day. I could not delay any longer but had to make the decision to leave.

I decided the town I would use to conceal myself was Urbana, Illinois, site of the University of Illinois. I had spent almost a year there with my brother and knew the campus and the town. Since many residents rented single rooms to students, I knew I could find an inexpensive room in some private home.

Meanwhile, since I would not be able to write directly from Urbana. I found a contact who could help me, a young woman living in Urbana named Marjorie Hissong, whom I had met a few years earlier while I lived in Urbana. I got in touch with Marjorie, telling her the same falsehood, that I was being assigned to high-level classes for the government at the University, but that I was forbidden to communicate directly to my home. The generous-hearted Marjorie agreed to be the transfer point for my letters home and, in turn, to pass on to me those letters written to me from Diana and my family.

When I left Chicago for Urbana, the farewells were all any prospective warrior could hope for. Wherever I went, I became the focal point of attention, a young man chosen for some highly secret and important service to our country.

The night of the last dinner I spent with Diana's family had her mother and sister embracing me tightly and crying unabashedly. As for the farewell between Diana and myself, never had lovers parted with so tender and gratifying an outpouring of emotion. With my ability to reconstruct and enhance the core of an experience, I actually began to believe that I was departing for some mysterious and immensely important realm of service to my country.

My farewells with Red, Jack, Chuck and Hance, my cronies at the liquor store, were just as heartfelt. My shoulder was slapped and my hand shaken numerous times. Chuck and Hance, brave, wounded veterans, warned me that whatever the assignment, never to volunteer out of false bravado.

I had purchased my train ticket for Urbana and told my family and friends that it was forbidden for anyone to come to the station to see me off.

In Urbana, I took up rental residence in the commodious home of a gracious family named Van Doren. I had a spacious attic room with bay windows looking out across the campus. The Van Dorens made me feel part of their family, allowing me to share meals at their table. In my room, I set up my writing table, determined to begin working on some poems and stories.

I'm no longer sure how many weeks I spent in Urbana living that charade, writing letters almost daily that I gave to Marjorie Hissong which she in turn sent on to Diana, my family and friends. They in turn mailed their letters for me to her.

In the beginning, Marjorie was my only friend in Urbana and it was she who began to take note of my misery. The deception was beginning to wear thin. I missed Diana, missed my friends and family. The absurdity of what I was doing began to dawn on me. The hours I spent each day reading, walking, trying to write, passed slowly and tediously. I began to consider seriously whether I shouldn't abandon the whole deception. Yet the immensity of my lie and the consequences that would ensue when everyone found out what I had done overwhelmed me. I did not have the courage to make that decision.

Then an opportunity presented itself whereby I might indirectly end the masquerade. I ran into a family friend who worked as a dining car steward and whose mother was in the same Red Cross volunteer group back in Chicago as my mother. I could have easily sworn him to secrecy, as well, because if I didn't, I knew he'd tell his mother who would unquestionably tell my mother. I think by that time I wanted to be exposed.

Less than a week later, I had a letter from Diana sent through Marjorie Hissong telling me my residence in Urbana had been revealed. Everyone was sorely confused. That same night I phoned Diana. We agreed that she would travel by train to Urbana. I promised her I would explain everything to her then.

Two days later, she arrived in Urbana with Naka as a chaperone. We all had dinner with the Van Dorens, and afterwards, Diana and I alone in the Van Doren living room, I confided to her my deception. I was grateful when she showed understanding and sympathy with the intensity of feelings that had driven me to the enormous lie.

In that moment, both of us in tears, I asked Diana to marry me. I'm not sure why I asked that momentous question at that instant. Perhaps it was an effort to pile drama on drama or an effort in some way to make amends. Whatever the motivation, I was delighted and grateful when she accepted. We resolved to marry the following year.

I left Urbana and returned home, telling all my friends that the special unit to which I had been assigned had been disbanded.

The war in Europe ended in June of 1945. On the 30th of September that same year, Diana and I were married by my father in my father's church. By wedding standards befitting the somber times, we had a small wedding with only thirty to forty people in attendance. The wedding that was to immediately follow our own, united a bride and groom from two prominent and wealthy Chicago families. As our marriage ceremony ended, the church began to fill with people attending the large wedding. We started our wedding ceremony with a handful of people and finished with a church packed in every pew.

Our wedding reception was in an anteroom of the church, a table set simply with Greek pastries baked by both our mothers.

Diana changed from her wedding dress afterwards, and our best man and his wife drove us to the Palmer House downtown. Although the war had ended, hotel space was still at a premium. However, through the efforts of a Palmer House hotel security officer I had met in the liquor store where I worked, we were able to get a room for the weekend.

In the middle of the night, my friend Red called, urged by our mutual friends, he said, to ask if everything was going all right? I told him to reassure my friends that all the requirements of a wedding night were being met. The lame conversation ended.

IN THINKING BACK through the years when I courted Diana, I find the memories dominated by the immensity of my lies. I try now to reconstruct my motivations. What amazes me is the ease with which I slipped from reality into falsehood. I also confess I cannot honestly recall feeling any remorse after the lies were exposed. The fact that I was able to conceive and follow through on the lies gave them, in my eyes, some moral justification.

I justified those falsehoods believing that a more beneficent result could be produced by my lying. As a youth I had performed in a number of the Greek tragedies. I had played Orestes and the Kings Oedipus and Creon. The roles I performed in my deceptions seemed extensions into plays of my own. In addition, I rationalized that I spared my family and friends the distress of learning I had been rejected for service. They not only felt better for me, but also felt better themselves.

St. Augustine wrote that God gave humans speech so that they could make their thoughts known to each other. Therefore, using speech to deceive people was a sin because it was the opposite of what God intended.

But St. Augustine also believed that some lies could be pardoned, those which did not harm anyone and which benefited others.

Thomas Aquinas felt that while all lies were wrong, there was also a hierarchy of falsehoods and those at the bottom could be forgiven. He distinguished between "malicious" lies and "helpful" lies.

How many times have we spoken falsely, "You look wonderful . . ." or "I'm happy to hear from you . . ." or "I'm sorry I can't make it, I'm busy that night."

I tried to rationalize my deceptions by recognizing that all of society is rampant with lying, "This product will get your wash 99% clean," "This car has only 20,000 miles on it," "I'm sorry, he's in a meeting."

Yet when all justifications and excuses have been submitted, a lie remains a lie and a society in which lying is acceptable behavior would be a society in which nothing would be believed. A simple phrase, "I love you," would be suspect.

At this advanced stage in my life, reviewing the decades since my prevaricating adolescence, for the most part I can't recall telling any lies of the magnitude of those I told in my youth. There is one exception, an infamous lie that looms over my head like the sword of Damocles. I will write of that lie in the chapter on my mother.

As for the lies committed during my efforts to woo Diana, I cannot in all honesty feel any remorse. If I hadn't lied, I wonder whether she and I would have married to have our sons and to live almost seven decades together. The lie about fencing and other mythical adventures kept her enchanted and our destinies linked. And when my great diplomatic service deception was revealed and she traveled to Urbana to join me, in the emotional turmoil of the revelation and our reunion, I asked her to marry me, and she accepted.

Without those lies, would the imposing blond Viking, Thorman, be calling her his wife now?

7

Arts Lunch

As a youth I often recalled hearing the reassuring aphorism that "all a Greek had to do to make money in a restaurant was to stand by the cash register and smile."

There was also a frequently asked question. "Why are there so many Greeks in restaurants?"

One of the most tenable explanations is that the early part of the 20th century brought an influx of young Greek immigrants into the coalfields and railroad construction camps of Utah and Colorado. These young workers were conscripted by a padrone or labor boss, who signed them into contracts that amounted to bondage in return for providing them passage and the promise of a job in the United States.

These young men lived in railroad cars and shanties. Sisters and wives had been left behind so the men rotated the cooking chores. Over a period of time men who proved more skilled at this rudimentary cuisine might have decided that cooking, as a means of making a living, was less hazardous than mining coal or laying track. The first Greek lunchroom was born.

As the owners grew more successful and their businesses grew, they brought cousins, brothers and uncles from the old country and put them to work in the kitchen as dishwashers. Once they grew proficient in English, these dishwashers were promoted to become waiters. When they had gained a measure of knowledge on how the business worked, they broke away to start restaurants of their own.

My experience as a Greek in the restaurant business came in the late 1940s, a few years after Diana and I were married. Since our marriage I had worked for a year in the U.S. Steel South Works and another year for the Simoniz Company, a wax manufacturer in Chicago.

A good friend of mine, Ted Christakes, a curly-haired, handsome young Greek, had been discharged from service in the Air Force and we discussed becoming partners in business. Each of us could raise about $1000, which even when added together, wasn't enough for a coffee dealership or a jukebox franchise we had looked at. We kept returning to restaurants, more precisely small lunchrooms, which better suited our limited funds.

We discarded the idea of pushcarts selling hot dogs and popcorn, feeling we could do better than stand out in the rain and snow to earn a few dollars. We inspected elegant establishments, which we couldn't afford, and some smaller establishments in working-class neighborhoods.

One of the places we visited was a modest lunchroom owned by an older Greek man whose last name I remember as Kanelakos. He had been in the restaurant business in half a dozen different Chicago locations for fifty years and felt it was time to retire.

"I've worked long enough now," he told us. "I've brought a number of nephews and nieces to this country and gave them a start. I wish now to return to Greece to die in the village where I was born and where my beloved parents are buried."

The lunchroom had ten stools around a three-sided counter and four tables. There was a circular-tiered pie case in which the glass had become so weathered and darkened by time one couldn't distinguish the different pies. A dingy, battered sign reading ARTS LUNCH hung over the front door.

Art had been the lunchroom's first owner in the period following the First World War and none of the four successive owners of the lunchroom had been motivated enough or had the money to put up another sign.

The lunchroom was located at 13th and Indiana Avenue, in a shabby but bustling commercial district that contained a potato warehouse and an armature factory. The lunchroom was also in proximity to the busy Illinois Central railroad yards at 12th Street and truck traffic also flowed through the neighborhood.

The first few times we visited the lunchroom in early November, the stools and tables were full. Two waitresses waited on the tables and counter while a cook and dishwasher handled the kitchen. The owner spent most of his time at the cash register and every time the drawer opened and the bell rang, it sounded to my partner and me like a Christmas carol.

Even this small establishment was beyond our means but the owner, generously willing to assist a pair of young entrepreneurs looking to get their start, adjusted his price to fit the cash we had available. In early December of that year, my partner and I became the owners of ARTS LUNCH.

Before turning over the keys, the departing owner issued us a warning.

"We are busy now because the factories and the railway express are staffed with holiday help." His voice turned somber. "But be warned that after Christmas, business will fall sharply. Then you must take care in what you buy and how you utilize leftovers."

Once we were set as owners, we realized that our zeal had obscured certain negatives. The stove in the lunchroom kitchen was a huge coal-burning behemoth that had to be loaded and stoked in the middle of the night so it would be hot and ready for breakfast. The icebox was a three-tiered, six-compartment wooden monster that looked as if it might have first seen service in the Civil War.

The sinks were two great iron tubs that were the domain of the lunchroom's main asset, a black man in his sixties named George. At the age of sixteen, lying about his age, George had enlisted in the U.S. Army and served as a bugler in the Spanish-American War. He was wiry-bodied, with alert eyes, strong arms, and shoulders stooped from years of bending over the tubs.

"George has served here since Art first opened the lunchroom," the owner had told us. "He sleeps in the storeroom back of the kitchen and gets up at four to put coal in the stove. All day long he washes dishes, cuts the meat, slices vegetables, scours pots and pans. He is worth three men in the kitchen."

At the end of our first two weeks in the restaurant, after all expenses were paid, there remained $600 profit for my partner and me to split. That was a 60 percent return on the $1000 each of us had used as a down payment and we jubilantly figured that even with reduced business, another few weeks would see our initial investment repaid. We congratulated one another on the sagacity of our purchase.

The first intimation of trouble came right after the first of January. Except for a modest influx of patrons at lunch, most of the stools as well as the tables remained empty from the lunchroom's opening to closing. At week's end we threw away a considerable quantity of spoiled meat and withered produce.

The trickle of business continued through January and into the start of February. Our weekly losses through waste and spoilage were staggering because we lacked knowledge and experience in how to reduce our purchases to match the dwindling number of customers. We also lacked any experience in how to utilize leftovers for soups and stews.

We let go our cook and one waitress. After trimming our menu to match my unexceptional skills as a chef, I retreated to the kitchen to handle the cooking myself.

In this time, coming to awareness that the restaurant could not sustain two of us, my partner and I flipped a coin. Both of us yearned for our freedom but I lost the toss and became sole owner of ARTS LUNCH.

I geared myself for a final offensive against impending catastrophe. I kept one waitress, a sturdy Norwegian lady named Maude, and relied on George in the kitchen. He worked double shifts that began at 4 A.M when he first rose and stoked the coal-burning stove. For the following 16 hours he managed the kitchen. I survived in the lunchroom only as long as I did because of his Herculean labors.

Predating McDonald's and Burger King by decades, I devised a lunch called "Burger in a Basket" which consisted of a burger, a few fries and a slice of pickle. For an aesthetic flourish I added a sprig of parsley. Our customers responded with enthusiasm but burgers alone wouldn't pay our bills.

Desperate times required desperate measures. We had been approached in the past by a scurrilous meat salesman we knew only as

"Sam the Meat Man." His rock-bottom prices and the wretched appearance of his merchandise suggested a slippery slope to food poisoning. (Once when we asked Sam why his chickens looked so dark, he reassured us with a guileless demeanor that the poultry had been raised on a farm in Florida.) His face beaming, he told us "those chickies enjoyed healthy sunshine all year long!" Our own somber assessment was that Sam's creatures had died of some poultry-related illness that we hoped wouldn't affect humans.

Frantic as I was in my struggle for survival, for the first time I bought a crate of turkeys from Sam at 15 cents a pound. I boiled those turkeys for hours and, when customers complained about the smell, told them a gas main under the restaurant had broken.

I served the turkeys all that week, varying the menu only slightly. Monday: *Roast young tom turkey.* Tuesday*: turkey and noodles.* Wednesday*: hot turkey sandwich.* Thursday*: turkey croquettes.* Friday*: turkey hash.* Saturday*: Chicken a la king.*

Despite showing a profit that week for the first time in months, those sad turkeys could not stave off my collapse. In the early spring, after a futile effort to sell the lunchroom, I tore out fixtures and furnishings that I sold to a restaurant supply house. The few hundred dollars I received was barely enough to pay the hospital bill my wife and I incurred with the birth of Mark, the first of our three sons.

In the decades that have passed since then I have resurrected memories of ARTS LUNCH many times to mine the experience for the writing of essays and stories. These have long since repaid my original investment and compensation for the time I spent as partner and then owner.

But the lunchroom also provided me an invaluable lesson in the diversity of human beings. Recalling that period of time brings faces and memories to me with a searing clarity. First among these was George who supervised that dingy kitchen as if he were the caretaker of an elegant Gold Coast establishment. Then there were the waitresses, Maude, Goldie, Henrietta, and the cooks, Gay and Chester. The procession of customers, some I came to know by their first names, factory workers, railroad baggage handlers, truck drivers, all these good people patronizing ARTS LUNCH in an effort to keep me solvent.

There was another group of visitors who entered and left by the kitchen door and were never issued a check. These were the hobos off the freights from the nearby railroad yards. From the beginning of our tenure in the lunchroom, we provided each of them a bowl of soup and a sandwich. That earned ARTS LUNCH a four-star rating in the *Hobo's Travel Guide* and every week that passed saw more itinerants stopping in the lunchroom.

They brought their slang and their stories of riding the rails, their struggles to elude malevolent brakemen they called "bulls" who beat them up and threw them off the train.

There were days and nights during that winter of the lunchroom, while an inhospitable snowstorm and frigid cold assailed the city, when as many as a dozen hobos lounged around our great coal-burning stove and then slept on the kitchen floor between layers of newspapers they called "California blankets."

Some had left home of their own choosing, others because they had been forced out. A hobo who had lived with three sisters told me his father had ordered his brother and him to leave because he couldn't afford to feed all five children. Another grim-faced hobo had ridden the rails from Oregon to the Midwest, pursuing a wife who had left him for another man. When he related the story he hadn't yet made up his mind whether to try and persuade his wife to come back to him or kill her and her lover.

There were also hobos who simply loved riding the rails. Sometimes there were places such as the Grand Canyon and Niagara Falls they wanted to see, but often it was simply the lure of the open road.

"When I hear a train whistle," a white-haired old hobo who had been riding the rails for forty years told me. "I can't sit still but I got to grab on to a car."

There was at least one doctor in that procession of transients, several lawyers, a journalist and a PhD in philosophy. Often they had been driven to their nomadic lives by the excesses of drink.

There was a blind hobo called Blinky, dependent upon the assistance of others to help him on and off the freight cars, and a hobo named Benny Guitar who had lost a leg under a freight car in Kansas City. For several nights in a row while a Chicago blizzard raged,

Benny entertained the gathering around the old stove with his guitar and his songs, and then he too was gone.

There were a few women hobos, mostly younger ones with strong bodies and faces weathered beyond their years, each one with her own tale of the open road. One was Molly who told me that when a railroad bull had tried to rape her, she had beaten him to death.

One trait the hobos shared was their ability to tell stories. As with Molly's story of attempted rape and murder, I was never sure whether they were telling the truth, but as an aspiring storyteller, I never cared much about the distinction.

Sometimes, if they passed George's stringent inspection, we put a few of these transients to work for a few days washing dishes.

One hobo named Denby had been a chef and for about a week he worked zealously preparing meals in the kitchen. His skill was apparent and thinking an improved cuisine would draw customers, I offered him a regular job. He accepted but after I'd paid him for several days' work, he left and didn't return for several weeks. When he came back to the lunchroom, his haggard face and red-rimmed eyes gave evidence he'd been through a bout of heavy drinking.

I was willing to forgive Denby and allow him to return to work but George wouldn't have him in his kitchen. Before he left, Denby made a final plea for a little traveling money, pledging to leave his knapsack as security.

I gave him a few dollars and although I didn't want the knapsack, he left it anyway. The battered cloth receptacle lay in the storeroom for weeks, but Denby never returned.

A few months later as we were selling off the fixtures, I opened Denby's knapsack. It contained a few articles of clothing, a menu from an upscale restaurant where he had cooked, several fine bone-handled chefs' knives and a small ribbon-tied packet of letters. I read several and then, wrenched by emotion, read the rest. They were from his wife living in a small town in Minnesota. Denby had left her and their small daughter to hit the road, vowing not to return until he'd broken his addiction to alcohol. His wife's letters pleading with him to return home traced his forlorn journey from city to city, ending finally in Chicago.

Moved by her letters I walked along Skid Row a few times to see if I could locate Denby. I checked other restaurants in the neighborhood where he might have found work. I also spoke about him to a policeman who ate in the lunchroom and whose beat included Skid Row. He pledged to keep an eye open for Denby but we never found him. I considered writing to his wife but didn't know how to tell her (or perhaps didn't have the heart to tell her) that her husband's journey had finally come to an end in the streets of Chicago.

8

Mother and Family

PART ONE

As I've grown older, images of my father have receded and memories of my mother have grown sharper. While I sometimes dream of my father I more often dream of my mother. That imbalance in recall may rest with the fact that my father died much earlier than my mother, on Memorial Day 1951 when he was sixty-six. I was twenty-eight and had been married to Diana for seven years.

My mother outlived my father by twenty-eight years, twenty-three of which she spent living with Diana and me. The last four years of her life until her death in 1979 at the age of ninety-one were spent in a nursing home. Through those final years I watched her great spirit slowly succumb to resignation and despair. I was the one responsible for placing her in the facility, a decision I feel guilty about to this day. Perhaps that is why I dream of her so often.

I once told a psychiatrist who helped me through a period of severe depression and who became a close friend that my decision to place my mother in the nursing home meant that I would someday end up confined to a wheelchair in a nursing home. His sagacious response was that I might indeed end up in a wheelchair in a nursing home but that it would have nothing to do with my mother. Nevertheless, the guilt remains and I try to appease it by being as caring to people in need as my mother had been. Her generosity was one of her staunchest traits. She not only exerted every effort to help others, her commodious heart caused her to suffer their afflictions with them.

MY PARENTS IMMIGRATED to this country from the island of Crete in 1916. They brought four of my brothers and sisters with them. Their destination was Price, Utah, a coal-mining community some 50 miles from Salt Lake City.

Shortly after the turn of the last century, young men from Greece and the islands including Crete, seeking a way to get to America signed labor agreements with the *padrone* or labor boss who traveled from the U.S. to recruit them. Their signature provided them steerage tickets to America with a guarantee they would be given work in the coalmines of Utah and Colorado.

At that time the mines were dangerous environments in which to work with numerous cave-ins and mine explosions. In these makeshift mining towns the young Cretans lived in shanties and boxcars. They labored long and hard hours to repay the money advanced for their passage plus accrued interest the *padrone* tacked on their debt. In addition they faced the resentment of Native Americans who saw them as untamed, their customs and their language strange and their conduct dangerous.

One such community of young Cretans in a town called Price in Utah had built a church but lacked a priest. They petitioned the bishop in Crete to send them a priest but they asked especially for a priest with a family. They had left sisters, wives and mothers behind them and they longed for the sight of a Cretan woman and Cretan children.

My father and mother had married in 1908, just prior to his ordainment as a priest and by 1916 had borne four children. My father had a fine parish in the island city of Rethymnon and had little incentive to leave Crete for the long, hazardous journey across the ocean.

But the young men in Utah kept writing and pleading, the Bishop kept imploring my father and despite Europe being at war, my parents consented to make the journey. In later years my father told me they made their decision because they knew that America would provide greater educational opportunities for their children.

Despite traveling second class which allowed the six members of my family a small but private cabin, the journey was tumultuous, several of the children being seasick for most of the voyage.

When their ship docked in New York, they were met by a representative from the parish in Price. They traveled by train west to Salt Lake City. From there they would go by car to Price.

Awaiting their arrival in Salt Lake City, unknown to my parents, hundreds of enthusiastic miners had gathered to greet the new parish priest. This was the West and the miners carried rifles and revolvers, which they used freely for celebrations.

In the Salt Lake City terminal, my family was greeted with a thunderous cannonade of gunfire. My mother told us later that she and the children were terrified, fearing they had entered a war zone until the man traveling with them reassured her.

My mother also spoke in later years of the silence that fell over the crowd of men when she and my sisters descended from the train. Tasula and Barbara dressed in white lace dresses and my comely mother must have appeared saintly figures to the lonely men.

As my mother and my sisters walked slowly through the crowd, men wept and whispered prayers of gratefulness. And a few, my mother told us, knelt and kissed the hem of her dress when she passed, so grateful were they for the sight of a Cretan mother and Cretan children.

My family spent about two years in Price They moved from that parish to a small parish in Savannah, Georgia. A year later they moved to a larger parish in St. Louis, the city where I was born. That same year, when I was about six months old, they made their final move to Chicago, where the last of the six children, my sister Irene, was born. Chicago is where my childhood began. Sts Constantine and Helen would remain my father's parish until his death in 1951.

AS THE WIFE OF THE PARISH PRIEST, my mother was a whirlwind of activity. She organized women's societies, led fundraising drives, sold raffle tickets and solicited ads in the church albums. Her efforts had begun soon after she arrived in this country in 1916. Within a few weeks after setting foot on American soil, and despite not yet speaking English, my mother became active in Liberty Bond drives. In the interval between wars, she worked with interfaith groups, charity drives, the Chicago Beautiful Committee and various other philanthropic organizations. When the Second World War broke out, she organized savings bond rallies and worked with Greek War Relief as well as with Russian War Relief. Her efforts received commendations from city and state officials as well as praise from members of congress. She collected these letters in a pair of scrapbooks that grew bulkier through the years. In her final years, when friends visited our house, she would bring out one of her scrapbooks to show the display of letters and photos. At those times I wondered pensively if I lived as long in the house of one of our sons as long as my mother lived with us, would I also pull out reviews and letters to show visitors?

What made my mother's energetic swirl of daily activities remarkable was that she carried a disproportionate amount of weight for her height of less than five feet. (Her energy and mobility somehow neutralize the word 'obese'). She accomplished these daily tasks despite every morning having to bind herself into one of that old-fashioned wire and loop corsets. Climbing the steep stairs to the Chicago stations to board the elevated trains had to be an ordeal but she remained undaunted. If she had weighed a hundred pounds less, I cannot imagine her achieving any more than those tasks she accomplished daily.

Among her other activities she directed dramatic plays that were performed in our parish. On several occasions I had small parts in these plays and observed that my mother as a director had a fine sense of dramatic suspense, and a gift for motivating actors without offending them. The plays were well received and other communities invited my mother as a guest director for their own productions. One year she rode the train from Chicago to Joliet, Illinois daily for a month while directing a play for a church group in that city.

All her life until her confinement in the nursing home, my mother's principal volunteer activity was the Red Cross. Not long after arriving in Chicago from St. Louis in 1923, the year I was born, she organized a Red Cross Bandage unit in my father's parish church that met regularly through her lifetime. The ladies in the unit continued meeting after her death. Shortly after she was confined in the nursing home, the Red Cross presented her with a pin commemorating 65 years of unbroken service.

I WAS PROBABLY no more than nine or ten when I traveled with my mother to visit an ailing woman in our parish. We rode a streetcar, my mother carrying a basket laden with food. At the end of our journey, we descended stone steps into a dismal basement. The shabby, solitary room where the old woman lived was littered with papers, magazines and piles of soiled clothing. The woman, sprawled in a large worn armchair, was obese with a weary, misery ravaged face. There were hideous sores festering on her heavy legs. As she recited her ailments, her voice became a drawn-out, anguished moan.

An affluent parishioner in my father's parish who owned a dairy had promised my mother that he would arrange for delivery of milk and eggs to the woman, a promise he had failed to keep. My mother phoned him from the woman's apartment, her strong voice verbally lashing the miscreant for his failure.

For all the years I can remember, my mother's efforts to help those in need continued unabated. At the end of each of our Sunday meals, she'd gather leftovers and prepare to take them to an impoverished family in our community.

At one point during the years she lived with us, she took under her benevolent concern a tiny frail seamstress living in a furnished room not far from our house in South Shore. The seamstress had been diagnosed as dying of cancer and my mother visited her several times a week, carrying leftovers from our table. I was conscripted into service to drive my mother for her visits to the seamstress, a task I performed resentfully because of the encroachment on my own time.

The seamstress lived in a mixed race building, young black children on the landings watching us silently as we ascended the stairs. Inside her single-room apartment, the seamstress wept as she embraced my mother. She was a small-boned woman, with tiny fingers. Her face was pale, her hair thinning and bleached some washed-out shade of henna.

The seamstress was in pain and when my mother asked about her pain relief medications, she told us she lacked money to refill those prescriptions.

My mother sent me to a nearby pharmacy where I had the prescriptions filled and paid for them. Later, on our drive home I lamented the expense.

"You know we have trouble paying our own bills," I complained. "Why should I have to pay these charges for a woman we barely know?"

But my mother was unrelenting in her devotion to the woman and, during several future visits insisted I continue to refill and pay for the prescriptions. When the seamstress's condition grew critical, I was also called several times to drive her to the emergency room of a nearby hospital.

The seamstress had a pervasive fear of ending up in a pauper's ward in the county hospital. She had once visited that hospital and found the ward in which her friend was a patient, overcrowded and neglected by the staff.

A few days after one of our visits, the seamstress died. After knocking on her door without receiving a response, a neighbor called the building janitor who found the seamstress unconscious on the floor of the apartment and called 911. She was transported to the county hospital, the very place she had feared to go, and where she died a few days later. My mother made the funeral arrangements and convinced several affluent members of our parish to pay the expense of the casket, grave, and the cemetery charges for burial.

Sometime after the funeral, my mother told me:

"You want to write about life, my son. This poor woman who suffered so much and who has now died, she is life."

My mother was right, of course. She understood that caring for the poor woman was the moral and compassionate thing to do. She understood as well that her dying was an experience to be absorbed into my desire to write. A few years after the death of the seamstress, I wrote a story titled "Zena Dawn" about a little seamstress who was dying, and a black woman who befriended her. When I sold the story, the amount the magazine paid me far exceeded any sums I had paid for the prescriptions and whatever cost of gas I'd used transporting her to the ER. That was a profit my reluctance and complaints did not deserve.

AN OVERRIDING MEMORY I have of my mother is of a woman who was articulate and strong, spoke her mind and did not suffer fools lightly.

If there was any faltering in my mother's character, that flaw was simply the intemperate love and devotion she had for the first of her children, my brother, Dan.

I have no doubt my mother's all-encompassing heart was large enough to abundantly love all her six children but Dan was the one to whom she was most fiercely attached. I am not sure whether that bond resulted because he was her first-born child or because he was the one most conflicted by tangled tensions and emotions.

Despite holding a good job in the Chicago offices of U.S. Steel, Dan always struggled in need of money that my mother sought to obtain for him. He spent this money on fine clothing, new cars, and squiring attractive young women on dates to elegant restaurants and to the theater. The old adage "a champagne appetite and a beer pocketbook" fitted my brother.

Perhaps part of Dan's frenzied need for money came from his childhood. A photograph of my parents and four older siblings taken when they first arrived in America from Crete in 1916 shows Dan, large-eyed and earnest. My family had known hardship in Crete and Dan was old enough to have absorbed the promise of the American Dream. For his own sake and I'm sure for the benefit of his family, as well, he yearned for fame and wealth. Yet, fulfilling that dream remained elusive. Meanwhile, my mother bore the brunt of his aspirations and his disappointments.

From childhood I recall hearing their confrontations, Dan pleading that he needed money for a new suit or a new pair of shoes. My mother trying to make him understand how difficult it was for her to provide him that money. During the period of the Depression, the funds my father gave my mother to run the house were meager. She had no other source of money. Yet she never ceased in her efforts to help Dan.

There were days when my mother rose early to make the rounds of loan companies from whom my brother had borrowed money. She'd offer the creditors some token sum, a few dollars as partial repayment against his debt and, at the same time, implore them not to garnish Dan's wages at U.S. Steel and cause him to lose his job. I can only imagine the abuse she endured even if, in the end, they acceded to her pleas.

When loan companies would no longer lend my brother money, my mother borrowed money for Dan from friends of our family. When she could not repay those loans as she had promised, these friends carried their complaints to my father. He came home humiliated and bitter from these meetings to confront my mother. I think these arguments and grievances deepened the alienation that I witnessed developing between my parents.

How far back those disputes about my brother began between my parents remains hidden from me. Although my father never struck any of my siblings or laid a hand on me, I recall my mother saying that when Dan was an adolescent during their early residency in Price, Utah, if he came in late, my father sometimes beat him. Perhaps that is when she first became overly protective of her first-born child. While I never questioned my father about those beatings, I find it hard to imagine my mother would lie.

That acrimony and tension between my parents saturated every aspect of our lives, growing worse over time. When the doctors advised my parents to take my younger sister, Irene, who was suffering from severe asthma to a dry climate for the winter, my mother, my sister and I traveled by Pullman sleeper train from Chicago to Albuquerque, New Mexico, where we lived for about a year.

During our time in Albuquerque, my brother frequently phoned my mother for money. Once when his need for cash became desperate, she wakened me after I had gone to sleep and had me dress and bicycle downtown to a Western Union office to wire my brother money.

Desperate to satisfy my brother's never-ending need for funds, sometime during our stay in Albuquerque, my mother cashed in the Pullman tickets my father had bought for our trip home so she could send money to Dan. When the time came for us to return to Chicago we made the journey on a Greyhound bus, my mother, my sister and I, sitting up for the days and nights of the journey. That episode added to my father's bitterness and grievance against my mother.

The conflict and tension between my mother and father cannot be encompassed and understood without integrating the role that Marie Constand, Naka, played in their relationship.

When she died in 1949, at about the age of seventy-two, Naka had lived with my family for twenty-five years. In her early thirties, fluent in French and German, she had been governess to an Egyptian official's family in Cairo, Egypt where she met a Greek-American businessman named Joseph Constand, (shortened from Constandoudakis) her future husband. After marrying, they moved back to the U.S. and took up residence in St. Louis where Joseph Constand became active in my father's parish church, for a while serving as parish president.

The single memory I have of Joseph Constand came during my adolescence when while visiting in Chicago he ate dinner one night with my family. I recall him as small in stature, a fine-featured, gray-haired, handsome man. He and Naka had no children of their own but adopted a son they named Alex.

I knew nothing about the relationship between Naka and her husband and only learned later from my mother that it was marred by frequent arguments between Naka and her husband, often incited by interludes of drinking on Naka's part. Her drinking infuriated her husband and on a number of occasions he beat her. After one of Naka's prolonged drinking bouts, her husband banished Naka from their house.

While my family lived in St. Louis, Naka had become friends with my mother, and after her husband had driven her from their home, she traveled to Chicago to seek refuge with my parents. She asked my mother to allow her to stay for a week or until she could find lodging elsewhere.

Despite my being very small I have a curiously vivid recollection of that initial meeting between Naka and my mother, Naka crying as she related her plight and my mother beginning to cry with her, as well.

My mother consented to Naka's plea despite my father's warnings that she was interfering in the problems of another family. Nor was he in favor of allowing Naka to stay with us, warning my mother "about the danger of two women in the kitchen." But after Naka had moved into our apartment, week followed week, without her making any effort to find another place to live.

My mother never asked Naka to leave. A few months after her arrival, my mother also took in Naka's son, Alex, who was about the same age as my brother Dan.

Having entered our house as a temporary refuge, Naka remained with us for twenty-five years until her death in 1949. During this period of time, despite my mother's staunch support and kindness in allowing her to live with us, Naka became my father's ally in his battles with my mother.

I am not sure why Naka should have turned on the woman who had befriended her. I can only speculate that perhaps resentment born of envy was at the core. My mother had a large family, and as wife of the parish priest held a respected position in the community. Naka remained an outsider living on the bounty of our family.

There was also a recurring tension between Naka and her adopted son. Several times I heard him condemn her bitterly because she had burned (she said on the orders of the adoption court) all photographs of his blood parents.

After a while, by common agreement, Naka and my mother came to terms by dividing the domain each one occupied. Naka ran the day-to-day routine of our house, while my mother maintained her social and community obligations. My mother did the shopping and sometimes left instructions for Naka to prepare the evening meal. On those occasions my mother was home, she usually cooked our dinner herself.

Naka's principal responsibility in my mother's absence was to care for my sister, Irene, and me, make our breakfast and our lunch, get us off to school, and see that our clothing was washed and pressed. For a period of about a dozen years, she also took care of us during the summer at the cottage in Fox Lake.

Naka's presence in our lives throughout my childhood and adolescence was as towering as a mountain. As Naka and my mother became further alienated, tension developing between them, I felt torn between the women I had come to regard as both my mothers.

Naka died in 1949, a few years after I had married. I was the one who found her the day she was felled by a stroke. My wife and I along with our first son, Mark, born a year earlier, had moved from our parent's apartment into a studio flat in the Kenwood neighborhood of Chicago. Each time we brought Mark to visit her, Naka bestowed the bounty of her affection on our baby son as she had lavished affection on me.

One of our final visits before her death was in my parents' apartment when we celebrated Mark's first birthday with Naka. We cut a birthday cake for Mark and I recall Naka's beaming face as she cradled our son in her arms.

Not long after Mark's 1st birthday, one afternoon after finishing my shift at the South Works of U.S. Steel, I went to my parents' apartment to see Naka. I was in the bondage of my gambling addiction then and a horse I had been following was running at one of the local tracks. Despite her own meager funds, Naka always managed to provide me the few dollars I needed. I visited her that day to ask her for money with which to gamble.

I still carried a key for my parents' apartment and when I used it, the inside chain obstructed the full opening of the door. Assuming that Naka had gone shopping or was visiting a neighbor and had left the apartment by the back door, I went downstairs and around to the rear of the building. The screen door of our apartment was locked from inside. Fearing something wrong, I returned to the front of the apartment and, with the door open a few inches on the chain, I rammed it with my shoulder until I'd broken the lock. I found Naka on the hallway floor, still alive but breathing hoarsely. My senses rattled, I called for an ambulance and rode with her in the ambulance to the Woodlawn Hospital, the same hospital my father would die in two years later.

Naka remained in a coma for three days until her death. During those final days I visited her for an hour or so, but quickly grew distressed watching her comatose figure lying still in bed, and I fled. As diligently as she would later look after my father, my mother remained steadfastly at Naka's bedside for those days before her death.

On the third afternoon having left Naka still in a coma, when I returned to the hospital after walking for a while along the Midway not far from the hospital, my mother met me in the corridor outside Naka's room.

"Where have you been?" she asked me reproachfully.

"Walking in the park," I said.

"She is dead," my mother said, and there were tears in her eyes.

Sometime later that evening as my parents began planning arrangements for Naka's funeral, I walked alone again along the darkened Midway. Naka had been wearing tiny red earrings and as I walked I cried and sang some makeshift, tuneless refrain about her dying "in her little red earrings."

Chapter 8

We held Naka's funeral in a small neighborhood Lutheran church with my family and a few friends occupying the first row of pews, thirty empty rows in the cavernous church behind us. The handsome young Lutheran minister who conducted the service and who had not known Naka spoke of having heard that she had been "a good and loving woman."

Her son Alex came for Naka's funeral from Akron, Ohio where he worked for the Goodyear Tire Company. It was the last time any of us would ever see him.

We interred Naka in our family plot at the Evergreen Cemetery, the first of the six graves in our family site to be occupied.

After all these years, I understand the influence Naka living with us for so many years had upon our family. Her alliance with my father against my mother imposed a hardship and suffering on my mother who endured that betrayal without complaint.

In addition, Naka spoiled me, impacted my childhood in profound ways, including causing me the anguish of that terrible summer in Fox Lake when she drank daily from June to September. In the end all these derelictions were swept aside by the enormous reserves of love she bestowed upon me. She could not have loved me any more fiercely if she had been my birth mother. She would assert in later years, as if it gave her some priority in my life, that while visiting my mother in the hospital on the day I was born, Naka had cradled me in her arms before my mother held me.

The image of Naka I sustain to this day more than six decades after her death is of a strange in some ways tormented woman, beset by superstitions, erratic judgment, and senseless fears, but also a woman who was devoted and loving. Even though I had by that time married and my wife given birth to our first child, Naka's death left an enormous void in my life. I felt that the earth was somehow more threatening and desolate for me without her.

Each morning during all the years she lived with us, it would be Naka's routine to prepare my father's breakfast. She would spread a napkin on the tablecloth and place his silverware, coffee cup and plate on the napkin. She'd make him his identical breakfast of oatmeal, coffee and a two-minute egg.

Since Naka died a couple of years before my father, it was accepted in our family that she had gone before him in order to set his table.

About a year after Naka's death, my wife, son and I moved in with my parents to occupy a house we bought together on South Ridgeland Avenue in the South Shore neighborhood.

I write that we bought it together but the $5000 down payment for the purchase came from the savings bonds my father purchased at regular intervals during the war. Those bonds comprised the only money he had ever been able to save. Although I contributed nothing to the down payment, my father listed us as joint owners.

For some years my father had been having trouble with a cadre of the wealthier trustees of his church. I haven't any idea how the friction began except that in our Greek Orthodox churches, dissension between clergy and laity wasn't unusual. A number of times the board sought to impose restrictions on my father that his independent nature resented. There were verbal confrontations between my father and Board members during meetings. Tempers flared and acrimonious words were hurled back and forth.

My father and the trustees were not evenly matched as opponents. The board consisted of wealthy, powerful men who because of their money could exert influence with the bishop of the diocese as well as with the archbishop at the archdiocese in New York.

My father was further burdened because of health problems. For some years he had been suffering from diabetes and heart disease. At the urging of our family doctor he had several times petitioned the board of trustees to grant him a sick leave. We had a fine assistant pastor in our church named Fr. Constantine Glynos who would have been able to assume church duties during my father's absence.

The vindictive board refused to grant my father that leave unless he waived his $200 a month salary for the period of time he would be away. Since that was money our family needed on which to live and pay our bills, my father could not accept such a condition.

Finally, under pressure from parishioners who cared for my father, and who thought he was being treated unfairly, with what we at first believed was a generous action, the board granted him a year of sick leave. They also pledged to continue paying him his monthly salary for the time he was away.

My father flew to California where he also made his peace with my brother Dan who had moved to Los Angeles to work for Columbia-Geneva Steel, a subsidiary of U.S. Steel. My brother was eager to make amends for the turbulent years and the friction he had caused between my parents.

Some years earlier my brother Dan had married a vivacious and lovely Greek girl named Penelope Siavelis. They had one child, a daughter, they named Barbara. For a few months they lived with us and then moved into a flat of their own.

After a span of years they separated and were divorced. A few years later Dan married a second time, an attractive and congenial Norwegian lady named Marvel.

When my father traveled to California to begin his year of sick leave, Dan and Marvel looked devotedly after him. The letters my father wrote back in the first weeks after his arrival in California spoke of the kindness he was receiving from Marvel and Dan. He also wrote of the glowing California sun. There was a letter to my mother that she shared with us.

> Each day that passes here I can feel the sun burning the poison from my body. Yesterday, after attending church, I went fishing with Dan and we caught enough for Marvel to prepare for our supper. I am truly feeling better and know I will be stronger when I return home.

However, within weeks of my father's departure on his sick leave, in an act of brazen betrayal, the board of trustees claiming my father could no longer properly perform his duties, brought another priest from Greece to replace him in his church.

My father received the news of his displacement with anguish and bitterness. He returned from California in the middle of winter to fight for his church and his livelihood, a battle that proved futile against those powerful forces arrayed against him.

The board sent my father a stern letter informing him that if he ceased any efforts to reclaim his position as parish priest they would approve paying him his $200 a month salary as a conditional pension for a year. At the end of that time the board would review the situation and, depending upon whether my father had fully cooperated in all matters the board deemed important, (including accepting unconditionally the appointment of the new pastor) would continue paying him that pension for another year. Following that, his pension would be subject to a yearly review.

I would arrive home early in the morning after working a night shift at the steel mill, to find my father sitting at the dining room table, papers and letters strewn before him. He'd ask me to sit with him and he kept returning to the letter from the church board with its draconian conditions.

"What does this sentence say?" he'd ask me. "What does this word mean?"

My father was assailed by frustration and a growing despair, frightened by the threat of his pension being terminated at the willful discretion of the board of trustees. My father's hope for justice faltered and his health declined.

On one occasion he called in a close family friend, a young attorney, Connie Pitt, to review his legal options. Since there wasn't any contract between my father and the church, my father was powerless.

I was present at that meeting and remember the despair in my father's face. I also remember the anger in the face of the young lawyer as he reviewed the hopelessness of my father's position.

"You know what you got, Father?" he cried in frustration. "You got skata! Skata!" "Shit! All you got is shit!"

In the middle of February, only a few weeks after returning from California, the city enveloped in snow and bitter cold, my father fell ill.

For almost a week my father was confined to his bed. Hearing he was ill, family friends came to visit. I have a memory of entering his bedroom on a day when there were a half dozen old Greek women sitting silently in chairs around his bed. I don't know if my father found their presence reassuring but I found their solemn, silent presence and mumbling of prayers as a premature deathwatch.

In the second week of his illness my father's condition worsened and he was admitted into the Woodlawn Hospital. For three months he remained in the hospital until he died on Memorial Day, 1951.

In those last few months of my father's life, my mother spent from morning until evening with him at the hospital, tending his needs and assuring that his many visitors did not remain too long and tire him. Whatever friction existed between my parents was banished by her devotion to his care. She came home late in the evening, visibly exhausted from her daylong vigil.

During this time, my siblings and I feared my father would not survive his illness but my mother rejected our gloom.

"When your father musters his spirit he has the power of ten men," she'd say to her children. "You'll see that I'm right."

I visited my father from time to time, but I found the atmosphere of the hospital oppressive and my father's pale face and weak voice distressing. I quickly grew anxious to leave. He understood the reason for my discomfort and never urged me to stay.

"You go now," he'd say, "and do what you need to do."

One of my father's regrets was that he had never mastered English as a spoken and written language. For years he kept a book of English grammar on the nightstand beside his bed. While we lived together, after he'd gone to bed and was reading his newspaper, he'd hear me entering the front door of our apartment. My mother would still be out or perhaps baking in the kitchen. I'd sit on the edge of her bed and visit with my father. Sometimes he'd ask me to help him study the English grammar text. I did as he asked, often begrudgingly, because it was late and I was tired.

Visiting my father in the hospital during his illness, eager to make up for my earlier derelictions, I picked up the book of grammar my mother had brought to the hospital and suggested to my father we practice his English. His response was the same.

"Not today, my son," my father spoke in a weak, low voice. "I'm a little tired. We'll read the next time you come to visit."

ON THOSE OCCASIONS when he could muster reason for hope, my father spoke nostalgically of California. If he became well enough to leave the hospital, his hope was for all of us, Diana and me, our baby son, Mark, and my mother, to move to that state.

"You cannot believe how warm that sun in California is, my son," he told me a number of times, repeating the praise he'd written us when he first arrived in California, "It is like the sun that shines above our island of Crete."

While we encouraged and supported that dream, as my father grew frailer and weaker it became clear that he would never leave the hospital. As he slipped slowly from life, his fine-boned face seemed to radiate a strange pale sheen. Any effort he made to smile seemed obstructed by a growing stiffness in his cheeks.

Near the end of the third month of my father's confinement, I returned home one evening from my afternoon shift at the mills. My mother had come from the hospital an hour earlier. Shortly after I arrived, a nurse at the hospital phoned asking that my mother return. The meaning of that call was clear and my mother made her cross. Afterwards we took a cab to the Woodlawn Hospital. I cannot remember whether we spoke or rode in silence on that brief cab ride.

In the hospital corridor a supervisor met us, asking that my mother not express her grief too loudly since there were patients sleeping. To this day I consider that request as a brazen and insensitive intrusion on my mother's grief.

We entered my father's room that was dimly lit with a single overhead light. My father lay stiff and straight in bed, his face partially hidden in shadows. When I walked closer I saw the strip of cloth they had tied around his head to keep his jaw in place.

My father had long-fingered, strong and comely hands that I had often seen in church during the liturgy emerging from the wide sleeves of his gilded vestments as he raised the chalice and the cross. Now those endearing hands lay pale and still outside the covers.

My mother walked to the head of the bed and bent and kissed my father on the lips, the only gesture of affection I had ever witnessed between them.

"Now he is at peace," my mother said.

MY FATHER'S WAKE AND FUNERAL were elaborate events held in the basement of the new church the parish was building on Stony Island Avenue in South Shore. His wake and funeral were attended by several thousand people that included his parishioners, as well as parishioners and priests from other parishes across the Midwest. The bishop came as well as the archbishop from New York. The board of trustees set up an honor guard of their members around his casket. Whether they were expressing grief or perhaps their remorse, I was tempted to denounce them for their hypocrisy. Knowing it would grieve my mother, I resisted an impulse to drive them away. I also knew that the board members had visited my father in the hospital and that he had forgiven them. I had no right to carry my resentment into his death.

My father lay in state for the two days of his wake, and, as was the custom with the funeral of an Orthodox priest, lay clad in his gilded vestments, a glass shield sealing his coffin.

My family came from across the country for the funeral, my sister Tasula, her husband John Thoman, and their family traveling from Independence, Missouri, my brother Mike and his wife, Carmencita, coming from his army camp in Texas.

My brother Dan traveled from California. Whether from lack of funds with which to fly or to prepare himself emotionally for my father's funeral, Dan drove alone from the West Coast. Driving those long solitary days across the vastness of the country, I can only imagine how his thoughts must have accused one another as he recalled the grief he had caused my parents.

During those days of my father's wake, men and women he had baptized and later in their lives married and whose parents he had buried, passed by his casket to make their cross and whisper a prayer. As with my mother's funeral twenty-eight years later, when she lay in state in our church, as well, many people paused to speak to my siblings and me, telling stories of ways in which my father counseled and aided them.

At the end of the funeral service, the procession to the cemetery contained several hundred cars. Unable to maintain any order in the jumble of city traffic, many cars were separated from the funeral cortege along the way. After my father's interment and the brief graveside ceremony, as we were departing the cemetery, a score of cars that had been separated from the procession straggled through the cemetery gates.

My father's net worth at the time of his death besides the small equity in the house we shared was a twenty dollar bill placed under his hospital pillow by a parishioner and friend who loved him named John Semedalas. There was also a $1000 insurance policy we collected at the rate of $100 a month for the following ten months.

There were rumors after his death that the parish might grant my mother a pension for my father's twenty-five years of service. This was at a time when priests had no designated pensions and social security had not yet been enacted. But the same board of trustees who had betrayed my father had little interest in making amends and that pension never materialized. For the remainder of her life my mother who had been left penniless at the time of my father's death was dependent upon her own efforts and the bounty of her children.

9

Mother and Family

PART TWO

My mother was a strong, moral woman with a rigid view of what comprised proper conduct and the place of God in our lives. While she rarely raised her voice, she was a resolute, imposing presence for our sons and for Diana and me.

In my family's homeland of Crete, as in the rest of Greece, it was accepted that an aged parent remained with the family to be looked after until his or her death. That was the proper thing to do.

Diana and I accepted that my mother's place was with us. She preferred living with a son rather than a daughter, and I was the only son still in Chicago. But as the years passed, her presence became more and more intrusive. With my mother often deciding what we would eat for dinner, and then often cooking those meals herself, Diana never really became mistress of her own kitchen.

The day-to-day life of our family also bore my mother's constant scrutiny. Every reprimand as parents we made to our sons or the smallest argument between Diana and me was magnified by my mother's presence. We were not allowed to go through the growing pains of any family without being under my mother's judgmental eye. However discreet she tried to be, her very presence altered the equation.

Adding to the general tension in our house was our constant need for money to pay monthly bills, a struggle complicated by my being so erratic a wage earner. I stumbled through a series of jobs that often ended after a few months by my quitting or, more likely, being fired.

I was fired from a job with the Simoniz Company, a manufacturer of auto waxes and furniture polishes, a job I had held for about a year. The hammer came down on the Holy Friday of Greek Orthodox Easter. After being notified of my firing, in a desperate effort to salvage a position that would allow me to hold a job, I visited several department heads I had come to know. We had bowled together and eaten lunches together. Each one was sympathetic but none could help me. I finally had to empty the contents of my desk into a small cardboard box, go home and convey the unhappy news to my wife and mother. Diana cried while my mother paced woefully back and forth, crossing herself, lamenting the timing of my firing, as if both Jesus Christ and I were suffering the ordeal of a crucifixion.

On Sunday mornings my mother always attended church and expected us to do the same. Our sons were also to assist as altar boys or attend Sunday school. If for some reason Diana and I decided not to go on a particular Sunday, my mother warned us of the baleful consequences neglecting our faith would have on our sons.

My mother's solicitude for others sometimes added burdens onto Diana. Among her volunteer services my mother listed herself as a Greek language resource for Traveler's Aid. On one occasion a Greek traveler who could not speak English arrived in Chicago with no one to meet him. Traveler's Aid phoned our home and my mother told them to put the man in a taxi and send him to our house. Meanwhile, she did not alter her social calendar and left Diana to care for the bewildered old Greek. For several days that he spent in our house, Diana made his meals, and initiated a series of cross-country phone calls in an effort to locate his family. I did my part by opening the couch-bed for him at night.

Throughout these years there were tensions in our house that could not be blamed on my mother. Feeling an urge to write stories, I tried to snare a few hours at a time to write. That desire to apportion some time conflicted with my responsibilities as a wage earner, husband and father, and those everyday tasks that needed to be done.

My day seemed bedeviled with numerous interruptions. Driving to the store for groceries, picking up one of the boys for baseball practice, taking my mother to church to meet with her Red Cross unit, all drained away the time I felt I should be writing.

What I wouldn't admit to myself was that I was the one most responsible for getting little done because I lacked the discipline to properly utilize what time I did have available. As days passed into weeks and I wrote nothing or else just produced a few pages, instead of placing blame on myself where blame belonged, I unfairly resented not only my mother but my wife and sons, as well.

TO HELP PROVIDE MY MOTHER FUNDS for her personal expenses, I arrived at an agreement with my brothers and sisters, that each sibling would contribute $25 a month toward her needs. For the most part, my family met this obligation.

My mother had no source of income beyond those intermittent checks sent to her by my siblings. She accepted those checks but her pride and sense of independence bristled. Determined to raise money through her own efforts, she began a business preparing Koliva, the boiling, drying, and decorating of wheat used in our Orthodox church services to memorialize the dead. As the wheat when it is planted sprouts from the earth, the Koliva symbolized the souls of the dead rising from their graves for rebirth and salvation.

The first large, circular tray of Koliva was prepared for the day of the funeral, another tray prepared for a forty-day memorial service, and then trays prepared again at intervals of six months, one year, and each year thereafter.

The Koliva business began slowly and thrived under my mother's zealous direction. Hearing of a death in our parish, she would be on the phone within an hour soliciting the family's business. If the family had already ordered their Koliva from some commercial bakery, my mother made no effort to mute her displeasure.

In an earlier book, I described the process of preparing the Koliva:

Like a secret rite of some aboriginal tribe, preparing the Koliva required the dried kernels of wheat be boiled for hours in great kettles of water. The starch from the wheat formed a pungent, bubbling crust on the surface of the water, which had to be skimmed off at regular intervals. This brew had to be stirred frequently with a long wooden spoon to keep the kernels from adhering to the bottom of the kettle. After the kernels had become tender, the kettle was lugged to the sink or laundry tub, the viscid, sticky water drained off, the kernels rinsed a number of times and then spread on large cloths to dry. That completed Saturday's labor.

Early Sunday morning my mother with my wife helping her began their labor again. My mother browned sesame seed and flour in a shallow baking pan while my wife lined a large silver tray with wax and paper doilies. The sesame seed was mixed into the wheat, and then chopped walnuts, cinnamon, shredded parsley, and sweet white seedless currants were added. This mixture was piled into a mound on the doilies of the tray. A half dozen boxes of confectioner's powdered sugar were sprinkled over the mound and pressed down gently with wax paper to make a smooth and compact frosting of sugar. A cross and the initials of the deceased were outlined in the sugar and then slowly and painstakingly decorated with tiny silver dragees, each one placed gently to avoid marring the smoothness of the sugar surface. That completed the labor except for the delivery of the tray or trays to church early Sunday morning in time for the service.

Those deliveries were my responsibility, a task I performed resentfully, fearful of gusts of wind, squalls of rain, a hole in the street, a reckless driver in another car unaware that if I were forced to make an abrupt stop, I might be inundated and smothered in a blizzard of sugar, nuts, parsley, sweet white silver currants and silver dragees.

When there was more than one tray, my wife rode in the back seat, one tray on her knees, holding the rim of the second tray on the seat beside her. A third or fourth tray required the assistance of our sons.

Parked before the church, one by one, I had to carry the large trays into the nave. Encountering parishioners on their way to Sunday services, I was riddled by anger and frustration feeling our occupation made of my family a cabal of vultures, a covey of ghouls, flourishing on the dead.

Through those years I came to hate the goddam trays of Koliva with a virulent passion. I despised every detail of the lengthy and grueling preparation. The boiling kettles filling the house with rank steam as if from a witches' cauldron. The tables spread with drying wheat, and the mute, resigned labor of my wife on Sunday morning. Finally, the humiliation I felt having to deliver the trays to the church where my father had served with honor as the priest, and where our family was known to everybody.

There was a Sunday when I had made two trips to church to deliver trays and then a third trip to take my mother. I returned home to find Diane, her face tear-stained, sitting forlorn in the kitchen. All around her was the littered kitchen, pots on the stove, raisins and dragees on the floor, powdered sugar coating every appliance and table surface.

I knelt beside Diana, swept by feelings of concern and compassion. I also felt a bitter frustration and a rampant rage at myself for my inability to bring in enough money so my mother wouldn't feel compelled to make the bloody Koliva. As I sought to comfort Diana, I cried, as well.

Despite the hours of labor through the weekend, and the cost of the ingredients, my mother's compensation for each tray was only $25. As with all monies given to her by family members at Christmas or on other holidays, she rarely used these funds for herself but purchased bank drafts for amounts as modest as $10 that she sent to needy relatives in the villages of Crete.

THOSE YEARS MY MOTHER LIVED with us became more and more difficult as time went on. It did not help that I was continuing to be driven by contrary ambitions and desires. Frustrated at my inability to craft a publishable story, I would quit writing for a month or two at a time. After a while, a sense of futility consumed me. I felt the passage of each day like the tolling of a mourning bell marking my accomplishing nothing and my future appearing hopeless and bleak. In my wretchedness, from time to time, as an escape from my misery, I returned to my adolescent habit of masturbation.

Diana who had been raised by a stern mother fell again into a submissive role with my mother, one she silently resented, as she came to feel resentment about my mother's constant presence.

In December of 1956, after ten years of submitting manuscripts, I finally sold my first story "Pericles on 31st Street" to the *Atlantic Monthly* and two years later in 1959 had my first novel, *Lion at My Heart*, published by Atlantic-Little Brown.

Seeing my work finally in print, while gratifying after a decade of futile effort, did little to increase my income and stabilize the economy of my family. In an effort to provide me more regular employment, my brother Dan prevailed upon a friend who was an executive with U.S. Steel headquarters in Pittsburgh to offer me a job as a junior level speechwriter. After making a trip to Pittsburgh for an interview, Diana and I with our two sons moved from Chicago to Pittsburgh where a third son, Dean, was born in 1958 in Mt. Lebanon, Pennsylvania.

During the period we were gone, my mother moved in with my sister Barbara who had married John Manta, a wealthy Greek businessman and they lived in a spacious house in South Shore. While we were in Pittsburgh, my mother phoned us almost every day and wrote us frequent notes telling us how much she missed us and especially how much she missed her grandsons.

My sister and her husband had three sons, Leo, Frank and Steve, and my mother found some comfort in bestowing her love on them. Into their maturity these three men remained loving, devoted nephews to Diane and to me.

The speechwriting position was one I loathed and very quickly became anxious to leave. Full of a newly published writer's bravado, after little more than a year in Pittsburgh, I decided against all good judgment to earn my living as a freelance writer. I quit my job with U.S. Steel, (thwarting by a scant few weeks the intention of my boss to fire me) and returned with Diana and our sons to Chicago.

In my reckless decision to become a freelance writer, we were generously aided by our Manta nephews. One of the properties their father, John Manta, owned was a once grand old house on 75th Street near the lake on Chicago's South Side. In the turn-of-the century days of gaslight elegance, the three-story dwelling with its striking stained glass windows had been owned by a wealthy family. By the time we prepared to live there, the property had been used as a rooming house for a number of years. The house was vacant, neglected and in sore need of all manner of repairs. Nothing had been done to it since the plan was for the house would be torn down to make the land available for a new building.

Snared into the romantic euphoria of their valorous uncle giving up a regular paycheck in order to write, my nephews prevailed upon their father to delay the demolition. Then we all joined zestfully in renovating the old house. We painted the rooms, sanded the floors, and repaired the electrical wiring and the plumbing. A carpenter my nephews employed in their father's industrial painting business nicknamed 'Ziggy' was of invaluable help in building, patching and mending.

Aiding the efforts of my nephews and myself at renovation were the Herculean efforts made by one of my closest friends, a master-of-all household functions, named Jack Murray. He had been at my side as friend and confidante since our adolescence. The house would never have been made habitable without Jack's skillful assistance. He was, at different times, carpenter, electrician and plumber, displaying an awesome talent for repairs in a dwelling many would have given up as beyond salvaging.

I have this vivid memory of Jack working one day on our primeval plumbing system. I was in the bathroom on the second floor, my son Mark in the doorway of the first floor, and Jack out on the street lying on his stomach turning the on/off water valve in the pit.

"Turn it off!" Jack shouted.

"Turn it off!" My son echoed.

Somehow, confused by the shouted instruction I neglected to fully close the water.

"Goddamit, I said turn it off!" Jack shouted as a geyser of water burst about him.

"Goddamit, he said turn it off!" my son shouted from the first floor.

As we prepared to move in, we understood certain areas of the house were beyond redemption. The attic and basement remained the exclusive domain of squirrels, mice and spiders. Despite these omissions, when the work had been finished, the grand old house sparkled in readiness for our occupancy.

For the following two years the Manta family enabled my survival as a freelancer by sparing us any obligation to pay rent. That proved a crucial benefit since my income the first year from the sale of several stories was around $1600 dollars and the second year somewhere around $2500.

We ate on the bounty of friends as well as our relatives, sharing dinners with Diana's parents several times a week. While my mother-in-law cooked sumptuous meals for us, her demeanor when she looked at me indicated she thought what I deserved was a dinner prepared by Lucrezia Borgia.

While continuing to live with my sister and her family in their elegant South Shore house, my mother also made every effort to assist us. After a lavish dinner party in the Manta home, she would phone me to come to the big house. In the pantry of the kitchen she would have set aside several shopping bags packed with butter, eggs, milk and cuts of prime meat.

While I recognized how much my family needed this assistance, I also felt resentful and embarrassed in my role as a poor relative. These feelings of shame and humiliation were intensified one evening as I was carrying two packed shopping bags from the kitchen to my car and ran into my brother-in-law, John Manta. Although he looked at me and said nothing, I felt as if I were a thief who had been caught carrying away stolen spoils.

When I vented these feelings to my mother she called them nonsense and cited the cooking and other food preparation she did for my sister.

"I do not ask nor do I take any money to help your sister," she said. "And I know she does not begrudge me these groceries I take for my family."

At the beginning of the third year we lived in the old house by the lake, John Manta sold the property to be demolished and a new structure built on the site. We searched for another place to live and bought a small stucco bungalow in South Shore. The price for the house was $17,000 and the down payment required was 20 percent or $3400. Since the most money I could raise was $1400, we were only able to buy the house because the real estate agent, a benevolent and warm-hearted lady named Tena Spira advanced us her commission to use toward the down payment. I was grateful for that act of generosity and, within the following few years, was able to repay her debt.

What became obvious after we had returned to Chicago was that my mother sorely missed living with us. Not long after we had moved into the new house, by unspoken agreement, we packed up my mother's belongings and moved her back in with us.

BY 1965, IN ADDITION to my first novel, *Lion at My Heart*, I had published a second novel, *The Odyssey of Kostas Volakis*, and a collection of short stories, *Pericles on 31st Street*. I had also been publishing a series of short stories in the *Atlantic*, the *Saturday Evening Post* and *Playboy*.

While the books and the lecturing I had begun doing supplemented my income, financial relief eluded us until the publication of my next novel, *A Dream of Kings*. For the first time I had the experience, so rare among writers, of watching one of my books become a best seller, finding a niche in the top ten best-seller list in the *New York Times*. The main prize came when the novel was sold to a Hollywood studio for a film.

Shortly after that movie sale, I was invited by the studio that had purchased the novel, to come to California to write the screenplay. We made plans to make the move, all of us celebrating except for my mother who, while grateful for my book's success, had her spirits darkened by knowing she would be separated from us once again.

This time when we left Chicago, my mother did not move back in with my sister. She was able to remain in our home when we found a young Greek couple from our parish with several children who agreed to share the house with her. We hoped that in our absence, she'd have the reassuring presence of another family.

But not long after we had taken up residence in California, reports came from my sister about conflict and argument in the house between my mother and the family occupying the house with her. There were disputes about certain items of food and how depressing my mother found the constant bickering of the parents with their children. I had no idea of just what transpired or who was to blame. I did know my mother sorely missed us and this may have caused her to resent the family living with her.

At the end of our first year in California, my sister wrote that my mother had slipped into a pervasive depression causing her to lose interest in all her social activities.

I returned to Chicago for a visit and found my mother resigned and despondent, for the first time in my experience sounding hopeless. She also poured out a litany of grievances against the family living in the house with her.

Before I returned from Chicago to California, we moved the family out of our house and my mother once again returned to my sister and brother-in-law's home.

WHEN WE RETURNED from California to Chicago in 1968, because of the commodious houses in the San Fernando Valley we had occupied, we had grown accustomed to living space around us. The city with its rows of dwellings set side by side seemed suddenly constricting. We knew the dune areas of northwest Indiana from childhood and, using the California movie money as a down payment, we bought a house overlooking the lake, in Dune Acres, Indiana, a lake and dune community about fifty miles southeast of Chicago. Within weeks after we'd moved in, once again, my mother moved from my sister's house to be reunited with us.

While she was grateful to be joined with my family once again, my mother was unhappy in the isolation of the dunes. As with Diana's mother who lived with us for a few months before her death in 1989, my mother missed the people and pulse of the city.

We had to travel almost fifty miles from our home to my father's parish church, which had relocated from Stony Island Avenue in Chicago to Palos Hills, Illinois, a suburban community south and west of Chicago. Sometimes I drove my mother from Indiana to church on Sunday mornings but the distance made the drive every Sunday laborious. There were instances when she prevailed upon someone in the city to come and get her for a social event but there were numerous activities she missed because of our distance from Chicago.

In the mid-1970s, our family entered a period of emotional distress. Our eldest son, Mark, an aspiring actor and writer, had struck out on his own and moved to California. Two sons remained with us at home, Dean the youngest and John, our middle son, that year a junior at Kalamazoo College in Kalamazoo, Michigan.

Early in that decade, John developed a malady that while puzzling to the doctors at first was finally diagnosed as hepatitis which he may have contracted a year earlier while on a student exchange program from Kalamazoo College to a university in Bulgaria.

At the onset of his illness, he was granted a month leave of absence from school to recuperate, and that was followed by a second month.

When his condition still hadn't improved, he was forced to drop out of college.

We took John to various doctors in Chicago and the diagnosis was murky. All agreed it was hepatitis but there were different opinions on the complications that were impacting his recovery. In each instance their prescriptions called for assorted medications and extensive rest.

As a consequence of the diagnosis, a once healthy twenty-one year old had to wake each morning under the shadow of an illness that might become worse or even end his life.

John slipped into a deep, consuming depression, spending hours a day sitting in his room or walking along the beach. Diana and I grew more and more anxious, and without any experience of depression, uncertain what we might do to help him combat that increasingly grave disorder.

Adding to our daily stress were my mother's mounting ailments, a number attributable to her aging. She still mustered the will to rise each day, to strap herself into her corset, but once she'd eaten a light breakfast there was nothing for this once active woman to do besides return to her room, spending hours leafing through old letters and photos or rereading Greek newspapers. The only variation for her on this daily routine came when family members or friends drove from Chicago and its surrounding suburbs to visit us.

I'm not sure at what point our son's illness, added to my mother's laments, became unbearable. Absorbed in my own concerns and in worry about our son, I had less and less patience with my mother's complaints.

As winter closed in around us, the bleakness of the season added to the tension. The summer flowers were gone, each day bringing a somber, overcast sky.

As the weather grew colder, a recurring complaint of my mother became that the house was too cold.

"Put up a little more heat . . . please put up a little more heat," was a plea she spoke numerous times. Yet the only way we could make her comfortable was for the rest of us in the house to swelter. We did put a small heater in her room that she placed at the foot of the armchair where she sat and read, and that she kept running all day long.

FOR SO MANY YEARS she had proven rugged and resilient, able to care for herself and to help ease the burdens of others. Now, assailed by the infirmities of age, my mother no longer felt in control of her destiny. For the second time in our experience, she withdrew into a deepening depression.

There was an evening when Diana and I were watching a production of Tolstoy's *War and Peace* on the PBS channel. The season must have been winter because a log fire burned in our fireplace. My mother came from her room and stood for a few moments in the doorway to the living room. She stood there silently, and, after a while, Diana or I may have asked her a question.

My mother answered quietly with a phrase in Greek, "*Eho mia apelpisia . . .*" that would translate into English as "I have such a despair . . ." Yet, in Greek the word "*apelpisia*" suggests something darker than depression, a resignation beyond despair.

I cannot remember what response we made to her comment then, but I don't think any words we offered did anything to console her. The phrase she spoke had been born in a depression spawned by her ailments and her age, a wretched and hopeless reaching out for some understanding that we lacked the empathy and experience to comprehend. We continued watching the movie and after standing in the doorway for another moment, my mother returned to her room.

What I could not understand then and only understand because I am at the age my mother had lived to by then, was the hopelessness with which she rose to confront her days. Her body had begun to succumb to the infirmities of aging, and she had nothing to look forward to but further decline. All the activities which had once provided her life meaning were lost.

Meanwhile, between John's illness and depression and my mother's failing health and her depression, day-to-day conditions in our house became harder and harder to endure.

I discussed the situation with my siblings and then with my nephews, who once again indicated their willingness to help. They and their wives lived in suburban areas closer to the city and nearer to my father's parish church than our house.

My nephews and their wives agreed to take my mother into their house for the interval of a month at a time. The only obstacle to this arrangement was that my mother would not agree to leave our house. When we tried reasoning with her, she remained adamant.

"I am too old and too tired now to be tossed from place to place," she said. "My home is with you. Leave me in peace."

At that point I once again resorted to a lie, larger and more onerous than any I had ever spoken before. I told my mother I had accepted a teaching position in another state that would again require closing our house and moving my family away.

I expected her to continue to protest. But, at that point, whether because she accepted the inevitable separation or because she no longer had the will to resist, she said quietly, "Do what you have to do for your family, my son."

At the beginning of the following month we drove my mother to my nephew Leo Manta's house. He and his wife Sophia prepared a welcome dinner and we laughed and ate together for a few hours. It wasn't until the end of the evening, as we prepared to leave, that my mother's mood grew somber. When I embraced her to say goodbye, her grief was palpable. As we drove away, seeing her standing in the doorway of my nephew's house, a cleaving of remorse swept through me.

For the remainder of that month, my mother lived with Leo and Sophia. They had small children and my mother enjoyed playing with them. But, for the most part, her routine of sitting most of the day reading letters and newspapers remained unchanged.

I had told her our move out of state was being delayed, so she was able to phone us every night to hear my reassurances that Diana and I and the boys were well and that John's depression was improving.

At the beginning of the second month we moved my mother into the house of my youngest nephew Steve Manta and his wife Dena. Within a week of that move, perhaps confused by strange surroundings as she rose to go to the bathroom during the night, my mother fell. To assure there were no serious injuries, she was admitted into the hospital. That confinement produced a series of tests that revealed she was suffering an assortment of medical problems.

After a couple of weeks in the hospital, when it was time for my mother to be discharged, the question became where to take her. Since we had told her we were leaving, bringing her back to our home was not an alternative.

My sister Barbara Manta, widowed some years earlier, had moved from the large house in South Shore into a downtown condominium on Lake Shore Drive. She agreed to temporarily take my mother and from the hospital, we moved my mother into my sister's apartment.

But my sister's condominium was small and she had health problems of her own. Still weak from her hospital confinement, my mother spent most of her day in bed. Even with caretakers coming in to help, looking after my mother became a task beyond my sister's physical or emotional strength.

Another sister Tasula and her husband John Thoman, living in Independence, Missouri, agreed to take my mother. About ten days before Christmas, my wife Diana and my youngest sister Irene flew my mother to Independence.

From the beginning of her stay in Missouri, my mother phoned us daily, repeating the same lament she had voiced during our stay in California. She missed us and missed our sons. In addition she complained about constantly feeling weak and ill.

The time was early December. My mother had always spent the Christmas holidays with us, our house full of her children and grandchildren. Our family albums are replete with photos of her during those holidays, sitting in a rocking chair before the fireplace, surrounded by a score of offspring. In stark contrast to those crowded gatherings, my mother spent that Christmas in Independence with my sister and brother-in-law.

A few days after the beginning of the new year, my sister phoned with the news that my mother had become ill once more and had been admitted into a hospital in Independence.

My mother was about 86 years old at the time, suffering multiple ailments. There were problems with her heart, with diabetes and with kidney failure. Her days in the hospital were spent inhaling oxygen from a container beside her bed. Several times the doctors told us they didn't expect she would live. But with the same strength she had used to combat life she fought her assorted illnesses.

Diana and I discussed the situation and the burden it imposed on my sister. We made the decision that I would travel to Independence to help.

When I arrived at the airport in Kansas City, my sister and brother-in-law drove me directly to the hospital where they had been giving Mother an additional series of tests. I spent the next two weeks in Independence, my sister and I alternating time in the hospital with my mother. Among the battery of tests she had to endure, my mother had to take a bowel x-ray. Afterwards, the nurses gave her castor oil to flush the barium from her system, so for several days and nights, her journey of agony was to struggle from her bed to the portable commode, shit, then get back into bed, a nurse and I struggling to help her. Unable to control herself, she would shit again in bed, the nurses having to change her and change her sheets, the routine repeated . . . bedpan, commode, shit.

The tests proved my mother clear of any major disorder but the tests also exhausted her and tore her up. Meanwhile she grew weaker and the doctors were beginning to doubt that she would live.

For those hours during the days and nights I sat with my mother, I often found myself unable to control my tears. I accepted her as an old woman with little to look forward to but those moments when she could hug one of her grandchildren.

One had to believe that dying would end her suffering. At the same time to watch her battling for life was to be forced to join the struggle because if her life was long, eternity was longer. Her struggle wasn't graceful because there wasn't any grace or dignity in illness and old age, but it was a struggle. While doctors, nurses and my sister and I were endeavoring to aid her, my mother was the one fighting the hardest. The old Red Cross veteran and campaigner of a thousand raffle ticket drives was battling because she never knew how to give up. Now and then when a nurse's hand touched the raw flesh of her buttocks, my mother snarled, proving the eagle had not yet become a dove.

By the time she was ready to be discharged, my mother required nursing care that residence at home could not provide her. Since Chicago was where most of our family lived, we began searching for a nursing facility in that city. That search was my responsibility and I settled on what I felt was a reputable facility in downtown Chicago. Since my mother had no private insurance our family would need to pay the monthly cost of $1200. Once again, my siblings and nephews agreed to help, each nephew and sibling contributing $100 a month to help make up the total.

Diana flew to Independence and brought my mother back to Chicago. My sister Irene and I met them at O'Hare Airport and drove my mother directly to the nursing home in downtown Chicago.

My mother's admission into the nursing facility that day produced a strange confluence of destiny with my brother. After losing first one leg and then the other to his diabetes, Dan's general condition worsened and he had been hospitalized. He phoned from the hospital in California to speak to my mother that first afternoon she entered the nursing home.

Listening to her speaking to my brother in a low, weak voice I recalled the years of his troubles when she had been a whirlwind of strength for him, moving heaven and earth to help him. At that moment, white-haired, grown deaf and frail, exchanging a few faltering words with her first-born son; she was beyond providing him any help. But even through the weak whisper of her voice, I sensed once again the fierceness of the bond between them.

Within a few weeks of my mother being admitted into the nursing home, my brother Dan died. He was sixty-six, the same age at which my father died. His diabetes had become lethal and required the amputation of first one leg and then the other. After a period when his health continued to decline, he passed away.

My mother never knew of my brother's death. During the four years she lived in the nursing facility, I would bring her imaginary letters that I told her my brother had written. I would read these fictional letters to her, each one full of auspicious tidings. My brother was in flourishing health, he'd been promoted at work, and he had bought a new house.

In the beginning thinking my mother might wish to see the letters and read them herself, I painstakingly composed and typed each letter, carefully forging my brother's name. When my mother no longer asked to see the letters, I used the same letter over and over, making up words and sentences, false assurances slipping seamlessly from my lips.

As my mother began recovering from her hospitalization in Independence, Missouri and understood where she was, she began to feel

Chapter 9

frustrated and imprisoned. She struggled against the confinement of the facility, demanding to be released. On several occasions as I emerged from the elevator onto her floor I could hear her cries. Each time it would take me a while to quiet her by trying to reassure her that the facility was temporary, that the doctors wanted to keep her under observation.

When I confided to an elderly, sympathetic nurse how much my mother's unhappiness and struggle distressed me, she sought to console me saying, "Don't worry, my dear . . . after a while they all quiet down." I did not find that bleak prognosis consoling.

My mother did not quiet down. On one occasion I was told by an aide that, strapped into her wheelchair, my mother emerged from her room to stumble to the nurse's station, dragging the wheelchair on her back.

During a number of visits I noticed that patients sometimes waited an unreasonable amount of time for an aide to help them. These delays were particularly distressing if they were calling to go to the bathroom. A number of times I summoned the nurses for other patients.

After a few weeks I became dissatisfied with the level of care my mother was receiving in that particular facility and began searching elsewhere. At the end of the second month of her confinement, we moved her to another nursing facility, Peace Memorial in Evergreen Park. This was a church-administered facility with an avuncular director named Pastor Dauderman. The attention and care seemed better but the atmosphere remained the same . . . elderly and sick men and women waiting to die.

The families who came to visit suffered with their elderly parents. As I wheeled my mother around the corridors, I witnessed other families gathered around aged parents. All appeared sad and all looked guilty as if having an elder in the home meant that in some way they had failed in their responsibilities.

Those years I watched my mother's great spirit succumb to the deadening environment of the nursing home were agonizing ones for both of us. I suffered but my mother suffered more. A number of times I found myself wishing she had died in the hospital in Missouri.

Throughout the seasons of the year, the visits to the nursing home were the same. I entered through a pleasant reception area and then walked down a long corridor where aged and infirm men and women sat in wheelchairs outside their rooms. They sat slumped, semi-conscious, sometimes moaning. From time to time one would call to me as I passed, extending a hand in entreaty, mistaking me for a son, a brother or a husband. Others just stared at me with a curious intensity.

I came to know a number of the patients by name and paused to speak to them before moving on to my mother's room, which contained three beds.

My mother's bed was the one closest to the door. For a while the bed next to her was occupied by a patient named Magdalina. For all purposes she lay in a semi-comatose state and then when the nurses transferred her to a wheelchair, she slumped in the same uncomprehending condition. Feeling sorry for the poor lady, I also wished my mother had someone in a bed beside her with whom she could converse.

Our routine during each of my visits was the same. I'd help my mother from her bed into the wheelchair. If the season permitted, I'd wheel her around the outside grounds, an expanse of grass graced with gardens that flowered in season. In winter, I'd wheel her around the corridors of the nursing home. After a while we'd settle in the cafeteria to have a piece of pastry or a dish of ice cream. Finally, we'd sit by one of the bay windows watching the passing traffic.

I'd try to coax my mother into a conversation but she was mostly unresponsive. After a while I gave up and we sat in silence. From time to time she might ask a question in Greek.

"How is Demetra?"

"Fine," I'd answer.

"How are the boys?"

"They're good," I said.

We'd fall back into silence, her eyes watching the traffic. A few moments later she'd repeat the earlier questions.

"How is Demetra?"

"Fine."

"How are the boys?"

"Good . . . very good."

After a while I'd wheel her back to her room and call an aide to help prepare her for bed. After I'd pulled the guardrails up on both side of her bed, her final parting words were the same.

"God bless you, my son."

From time to time my sister Irene visited my mother, and on occasion one of my nephews or their wives. When my siblings who lived in other cities visited Chicago, they stopped in to see her. But the great number of friends she'd had when she was active in the community, all those men and women she had worked with and befriended, never again saw her alive.

I did not blame them. If she hadn't been my mother, I'm sure I would have avoided going to the home, as well. The atmosphere of those corridors where people waited to die was one of hopelessness and despair.

Diana and I visited more often than anyone else but the trip from Indiana, especially in winter, was long and we didn't go as often as we might have.

There were times when guilt spurred me to make the drive into Evergreen Park. I recall a lovely summer afternoon in Indiana, the lake water blue, laughter coming from the beach. We sat in the serenity of the sun-suffused terrace when I had a sudden chilling image of my mother slumped in her wheelchair in the corridor outside her room. Haunted by the image, I drove in to Evergreen Park to spend a few hours with her.

I sought to compensate for the span of time between my visits by hiring part-time aides at Peace Memorial to look out for her. After finishing their regular shifts, the aides would spend an hour or so with my mother, making sure she ate her dinner and then helping get her ready for bed.

One of the gentlest, kindest of these caretakers was a tiny lady named Gertrude Zatko. She would phone each evening before leaving her shift to reassure me that my mother had eaten well and was tucked safely into her bed.

Gertrude Zatko was with my mother the afternoon she died. That occurred on a day in early May of 1979. Diana and I had visited her the evening before, bringing her a small bag of the White Castle hamburgers she enjoyed. Early the following morning, for reasons no one knew, she tried to climb around the guardrails of her bed, and she fell.

When Pastor Dauderman phoned us, Diana and I drove to the home. My mother lay in bed, apparently not conscious, yet seeming to understand we were there. She pressed my hand slightly in response to my own hand. When I asked her how she was feeling, she whispered a complaint about a pain in her stomach. After a moment she slipped into unconsciousness again. Diana and I stood on either side of her for a while, holding her hands. An hour or so later we left the nursing home to drive back to Indiana. Not long after we had arrived home, Gertrude Zatko called to tell us that while sitting beside my mother, holding her hand, my mother died.

I wished we had remained with my mother a few hours longer. Perhaps I feared she was going to die and while part of me felt I should stay, another part longed to be spared that instant of her departure from life. It fell to the gentle little Gertrude Zatko to be the last person to see my mother alive.

In the Greek Orthodox Church only members of the clergy or the most prominent laymen were allowed to lie in state in church. This privilege was rarely granted for any woman regardless of her position. Once again, as she had done so many times before, my mother broke that glass ceiling. The church clergy and trustees decreed that she would lie in state as my father had been waked, encased in her coffin before the sanctuary.

For the two days of her wake, hundreds of parishioners passed her coffin, pausing to make their cross and to kiss the icon placed on her chest. Many paused to tell me stories of my mother's kindness.

"Two weeks when I was in the hospital," a man said, "she visited me faithfully every day."

"When my son got in trouble for stealing," a woman said, "she helped get me an attorney and came to court to sit beside me."

"We were doing our play *Golfo*," a woman who had traveled to Chicago from Joliet told me, "and your mother took the train from Chicago every day for a month to direct us in our rehearsals."

One old family friend made his cross and, with tears in his eyes, said quietly.

"This is the only time in my life I've ever seen this woman when she didn't try to sell me a raffle ticket or a page in a church album."

After her funeral, which had every pew in the church occupied and men and women standing along the walls of the nave, we drove in a long funeral cortege to the cemetery. In a brief graveyard ceremony, my mother was interred in our family plot, beside my father's grave and the grave of the son she loved and struggled to help so many times.

For a while I felt bitter about the disparity between the outpouring of admiration and love my mother received after her death and the silence of all those friends during her final desolate years in the nursing home.

As I grew older I came to understand that is the way of life. Men and women have their own sorrows, struggle with their own problems. One has to be bonded by blood to enter that bleak terrain of the infirm and the dying. If they chose not to visit her, that did not mean they lacked empathy or love.

My own experience confirmed that truth. Since I had come to know a number of the patients at Peace Memorial I vowed I'd visit at least once every month to buoy their spirits. But after my mother's death I never returned to the nursing home again.

WITH EACH YEAR I'VE LIVED since my mother's death, my age now near her age when she died, I've come to realize not only the force of her spirit and of her heart but also how much of her made me who I am.

Above all other things, she passed on to me a fragment of her mighty and compassionate heart, which through the years I have written has provided me empathy into the frailties of human beings. Even as her body weakened and she succumbed to illness and age, her heart and spirit radiated a searing force. To this day I can hear the softness of her voice as I bent over her bed to tell her goodbye.

"God bless you, my son."

But there is another memory about my mother that will haunt me for as long as I live. Once, during the years she lived with us, after some emotional turmoil in our house complicated by my mother's presence, while driving later that day into Chicago with my wife, I cried out, "Why won't she die!"

Stephen Dedalus, that complex creation of Joyce, bore the guilt of refusing to take communion as his dying mother beseeched him to do. My sacrilege was worse, when in one intemperate oath, I wished my mother dead.

Those four words have returned to ravage me a number of times in the years since my mother's death. As I write them now, they pierce into me once more. I have no doubt that her great, compassionate heart would forgive me but that doesn't erase my betrayal. If I am allowed to comprehend the final moments of life preceding my own death, I will ask her forgiveness one last time.

Petrakis family photograph from 1920. From left: Dan, Barbara, Tasula, Manuel, Presbytera Stella, and Rev. Mark. (An eight-foot tall replica of this photograph hangs in the Museum of Immigration at Ellis Island, N.Y.)

Left: Harry Mark Petrakis in 1925.

Below: Petrakis family photograph from late 1929. From left: Tasula, Rev. Mark, Dan, Manuel, Barbara and Presbytera Stella. In front: Irene and Harry Mark.

Seventh grade class at Koraes School in 1938. Harry Mark
at top left. His sister, Irene, at left desk, first row.

Harry Mark in beard as Oedipus the King in a St. Constantine's
Koraes School production from about 1937.

Harry Mark and Diana Perparos on their wedding day,
September 30, 1945.

Above: Petrakis family from left: John, Harry Mark, Mark, Diana, and Dean in 1960, after moving from Pittsburgh to Chicago for Harry Mark to begin life as a freelance writer.

Left: Harry Mark in the 1960s.

Petrakis family from left: Mark John, Harry Mark, Dean,
and Diana in 1969, upon their return from California.

Petrakis family from left: Mark John, Diana,
Harry Mark, and Dean in 1974.

Harry Mark teaching in the 1970s.

Harry Mark and Diana in 1990.

Petrakis family from left: Linnie, John, Lucas, Harry Mark, Diana, Nicholas, Dean, Adriana, Anna, Mark, and Alexis in July, 2005

10

Depression

My illness and the lethal depression, which followed and almost ended my life, began in late 1982. I had a minor surgery on my knee as a result of an injury I incurred while playing tennis. A week after the surgery I was lunching with a friend. When I rose to leave the restaurant, my right foot made a curious flapping sound as it touched the ground. I also felt a weakness in my ankle. I had never experienced such an affliction before and I was bewildered and frightened.

My first thought was that the symptoms were linked in some way to my recent surgery. When I phoned the surgeon, he had me come at once to his office. After examining me he determined the drop foot had nothing to do with the surgery. He surmised that while I sat cramped in the restaurant booth, my leg had been pressed against a wall. A nerve had been compressed and I had developed a drop foot. As a precaution, he sent me to a neurologist for an EMG, an electromylogram, an uncomfortable procedure in which small needles prick the flesh and record the nerve impulses onto a machine that the neurologist is monitoring.

Several days later when we had the test results, my surgeon phoned me, his voice somber, to tell me the test had registered "abnormal." When I asked for a more specific diagnosis, he spoke of a "sensory-motor neuropathy."

As a relatively healthy 60 year old, who had not been ill since my childhood bout with TB, I was suddenly hurled into a forest of speculation. Just what did "sensory-motor neuropathy" mean? What made any diagnosis difficult to pin down in specifics was that we were drifting in the murky recesses of neurology.

My diagnosis started me on a futile pursuit of the neurologists in an effort to understand just what those somber words meant and what course the affliction might take.

One neurologist told me I would be fine. When I pressed him about treatment, he told me there was little we could do. The neuropathy would cause a slow decline in my muscle strength and sensory perception. The more I tried for a clearer timetable on the course of the disease, the more elusive the neurologists became. I became convinced they were hiding some even more baleful information from me. As I became more anxious, one of the neurologists impatiently diagnosed that my problems were mental and recommended I see a psychiatrist.

In the following few months, I made appointments with and saw several psychiatrists. What I found most frustrating was that they regarded my anxiety as though it were unrelated to my diagnosis and needed to be treated as a separate affliction. I felt the neuropathy diagnosis and my anxiety were inextricably linked. I hadn't been aware of any specific psychological problems before hearing the dreaded "sensory-motor neuropathy."

For years in my writing and in my conversation with friends, I interjected references to Greek heroes and Greek deities. They were part of my historical legacy and my dialogue often included mention of them.

At the end of one session with a psychiatrist during which I referenced one or another Greek deity, the psychiatrist asked me gravely if "anyone else in my family suffered from megalomania?"

The uncertainty about what lay ahead began to impact my sleep, and my nights became fitful and rife with vivid dreams. Various sleeping medications were now added to the mix. Yet, fed by my own volatile imagination my anxiety continued to mount.

During these fretful months I was helped by an internist, Dr. Peter Economou, who also became a friend. In numerous ways, he sought to reassure me that I would be all right. But in my heightened emotional state, all his earnest efforts served only to convince me that some dire outcome was being hidden. The same fluidity of imagination that allowed me to construct my novels and stories turned malignant when directed upon myself. My fantasies concocted one gruesome scenario after another.

As my anxiety worsened, one psychiatrist suggested I undergo a series of electroshock treatments. Another recommended I enter the psychiatric ward of a hospital for several weeks.

These psychiatrists had also been prescribing strong antidepression medication, which caused a severe rash to break out across my back and arms. Standing naked before my mirror at night examining the hideous surface of pimples and scarlet scabs on my body further added to my anxiety. I felt myself turning into some form of monster.

When I complained to the doctors about the rash inducing medications, the prescription was "increase the dosage!" I did reluctantly increase the dosage, which then produced a new devil, an enlarging of my prostate. I began having difficulty urinating. This condition became so severe over several weeks that I became completely blocked and had to be taken to the ER to be "catheterized."

Finally, one dreadful night after visiting my family doctor who catheterized for the second time, I returned home only to find I had become blocked again. Sitting in a warm tub of water proved futile. After a night of excruciating discomfort, the following morning I was admitted into Rush-St. Luke's Hospital in Chicago.

Since my prostate had become significantly enlarged, surgery to shave it down was recommended. The surgery and recovery procedure would require a hospital stay of about three weeks.

Meanwhile, enduring those days of waiting for the surgery, then the operation itself, and the weeks of convalescence that followed, gave me ample time to consider my afflictions. A sense of hopelessness imbued my thoughts. The guilt and remorse I felt about things I had not done or should have done seemed to confirm my worthlessness as a human being. I felt I deserved whatever bleak fate lay before me.

I was visited almost daily by one or the other of my neurologists who, in answer to my persistent queries as to what the course of my neuropathy might be, remained noncommittal.

For the first time, one of them I had angered by my writing what he felt to be a flippant and disparaging letter and copying several of the other physicians, bluntly told me that what the other neurologists weren't telling me was that I was afflicted with the beginnings of ALS, the dreaded Lou Gehrig's disease.

I was stunned and asked if that diagnosis proved true, how much time I might have before I became hopelessly crippled. This same neurologist told me I would have "about a year."

After his diagnosis, my anxiety took a leap into frenzy. I felt trapped in the wreck of my decaying body. At night, despite the sleeping medication, I could not sleep.

In those tormented hours, listening to the night sounds of other patients, the moaning and the crying, I made the decision I would not wait passively for the crippling decay of my disease. I would not subject my wife and sons to that horror. In that solitary hospital room with a window that looked out across the terrain of the city where I had grown up and lived for sixty years, I resolved to end my life.

In the early 1930s, my father had taken a gun from one of his parishioners threatening suicide. The gun had remained in my father's possession for 20 years until his death in 1951, when I inherited the weapon. For another 30 years the gun had been stored in a small suitcase in my closet.

At that point I saw the weapon as the means of my liberation. There was even a dark irony in that after a hiatus of 50 years; the gun would finally serve its original purpose.

During the weeks I spent in the hospital, Diana took the train from Indiana every morning to Chicago to spend the day with me. Because I worried about her returning home by train at night, a dear friend, Gladys Wolff, came to our aid, allowing Diana to stay with her in her downtown apartment only a few miles from the hospital.

Diana came to the hospital in the late morning and spent all day with me, patiently absorbing the brunt of my depression and my despair. I cherished those hours we spent together that were made even more precious as I continued to plan for my own death.

I was also visited regularly by our son John who lived in Chicago and several times by our sons Mark and Dean who came from California.

During my hospital confinement, Dean, our youngest son had sent me a card which contained a haiku that he wrote had helped him at a difficult juncture in his own life. The haiku read: "Someday I may look back on this time when I am so unhappy and remember it fondly." Even as I felt the sentiment meaningless for someone who had so short a time to live, I began reciting the haiku during my recovery from the surgery, while I walked the hospital corridors. At night, tense and sleepless, I whispered the verse until I had repeated it hundreds and thousands of times.

Meanwhile, after my surgery and during my period of convalescence, I became a legend in the corridors of my floor at the hospital. Doctors and nurses commented on the skinny-shanked old man in his robe and slippers pushing a urinary pole as he circled the floor, twenty, thirty and fifty times a day. Many marveled and spoke of my perseverance and resolve to get well. What they didn't understand was that my passion and apparent resolve to get well had nothing to do with courage or bravado but was driven by sheer terror and desperation that had me circling that hospital corridor for hours at a time.

WHEN I WAS RELEASED from the hospital, my exercise regimen had helped heal my surgery. But my depression had worsened and I began to plan more precisely for my suicide.

I started a search for and found a small furnished apartment in Chicago into which I planned to move Diana so that, following my death, she would not be left in the isolation of the Indiana dunes. I told her the reason for the move would be to bring me closer to my doctors.

We located that apartment by a fluke, further convincing me that the deities were supporting the decision I had made to end my life. Dialing the phone in response to a newspaper ad for an apartment, I got a wrong number. The man who answered corrected me but when I mentioned that I was looking for an apartment, he told me a neighbor down the hall had a furnished apartment for rent. I phoned the number he gave me and the owner turned out to be a young Greek lady, Tereza Hadjipavlou. By sheer chance, she knew my family and had several of my books in her library. She had us over for tea and we signed a lease to rent her apartment. I marveled how fortuitously fate was assisting my design.

In November of 1983 we moved from Indiana into the one-bedroom apartment on Lake Shore Drive with a panoramic view of the lake and park at Belmont Harbor. At the time the landscape had descended into winter. The season seemed to fit my mood and, despondent and resigned, I moved closer to my death.

At night, lying sleepless beside Diana, I struggled to find some alternative solution that might save me. But the doors all seemed to be closing. If I didn't act soon, I feared a day might come when I would no longer be able to control my own fate. The final shattering image I had was of being slumped in a wheelchair, unable to eat or drink, dependent upon others to help me urinate or defecate.

When the pattern of cold was broken by a more temperate day, I walked along the lakefront. From that vantage point I looked back at the towers of the city, the line of apartment buildings. I thought of the families that occupied those apartments, living their own griefs and joys. I thought of Diana in our small apartment and what life would be like for her once she was alone. As I walked, I cried then, for Diana and for myself and for our lost love.

Another aberrant thought came like a knife-thrust into my plans. Instead of using the gun only to kill myself I would carry the weapon into the hospital Department of Neurology (I'd make an appointment first) and then kill my neurologist. Even better, I would endeavor to get more than one of the heartless wretches together so I could kill both. A novel I had completed the year before with the title *Days of Vengeance,* had just been published. I projected the newspapers grasping eagerly at the association. Riding the waves of notoriety, the author a murderer, the book might even become a best seller, providing Diana a bounty she wouldn't have otherwise.

That bloody and melodramatic course of action glittered enticingly for a few days and then was discarded for numerous reasons. I didn't know if I came face to face with my doctors whether I'd be capable of killing anyone. Then I didn't relish the prospect of spending the final months of my crippling disease in prison.

About a month after we'd moved into the city apartment, an opportunity presented itself for me to fulfill my suicide. I was on a lecture trip to a college in Wisconsin and scheduled to return home that evening. I phoned Diana from Wisconsin to tell her the lie that because of bad weather, my flight had been cancelled and I would be delayed returning until the following day.

Meanwhile, I flew into Chicago that night as originally scheduled, planning to pick up my car at the airport and drive to our home in Indiana. The gun was hidden there. I would spend the night writing final letters to my wife and sons and then end my life in those dune and lake surroundings I loved.

Since my wife expected a phone call from me when I was settled in my Wisconsin hotel room, I phoned her from O'Hare Airport after I'd landed. I planned to tell her I was still in Wisconsin spending the night in a dormitory room that had no phone so she wouldn't be able to phone me back.

When she answered the phone, her voice conveying warmth and love, my resolve to end my life faltered. Suddenly I longed for a few more precious hours with her before the end. I told her that I had managed to catch my original flight after all, and that I had just landed at O'Hare. I picked up my car from the parking garage and drove home.

If a moment of greatest despair could be measured, a time when I came closest to taking my life, it was that night when a phone call and Diana's endearing voice saved me. And it was from that dark night that I began a tenuous ascent to recovery.

My healing was slow, a few fragile steps forward followed by a lurching retreat while I continued to fight anxieties and fears. During this period, three doctors proved life sustaining. Dr. Peter Economou at Rush-St. Lukes hospital who had absorbed and cushioned my laments during my months of terror, continued to help me. Dr. Nicholas Vick, a neurologist at Evanston Hospital reassured me that my neurological problems had been with me since adolescence and would remain with me but were in no way fatal and certainly not ALS.

For a while I would not believe him, thinking his diagnosis was part of the pattern of false reassurance I had endured for so long. My anxieties remained, but were tempered by my new resolution that I would wait for whatever my fate might be.

Meanwhile, the soft-spoken, wonderfully empathetic psychiatrist, Dr. Sanford Weissblatt helped me mend the emotional excesses and curb the perversity of imagination that turned malignant when focused on my own psyche. Slowly I returned to life and hope.

My wife, Diana, and our sons, were my life support. Their unceasing love and concern gave me reason to look forward to each day. Writing helped me, as well, as I returned slowly to the routine of fashioning words into stories even as I wondered at what point my affliction might prevent me from any writing.

All this turmoil and struggle while I courted and planned for death, took place almost thirty years ago. Had I ended my life then, I would have missed the bounty of these last three decades. The marriages of our sons, from whom we acquired loving daughters, as well, the birth of additional grandchildren, family parties and celebrations with friends on summer afternoons and autumn evenings. Travels to Europe and to Asia, witnessing the rich diversity of other cultures. Finally, managing to write and publish additional books as part of my legacy.

Meanwhile, the haiku sent to me so many years ago by my son, Dean has proven true. If I do not remember the despair and desperation of that fearful time fondly, I do remember it gratefully. It made me realize what a precious gift is the luminous interval between birth and death we call life and how we must cling to it as tenaciously as we can.

Having my own life salvaged by the love of family and friends, as I write these words now, I implore troubled men and women and especially the young, not to give up hope. No despair is beyond redemption. In the final analysis, reasons to live surpass reasons to die.

Think, first of all, of those closest to you, those who love you and who would be most affected by your death. Spare them the pain. Death will come in its time but it should not be hurried. In the words of a character in a fine Chekhov story, "better to be last among the living than first among the dead."

There are blessings available to everyone that have nothing to do with the acquiring of wealth, fame and power, blessings the poet Homer wished for his friends. These are available to the young and the old, the weak and the strong, the cowardly and the brave. They are reason to live.

The old blind bard enjoins us to find our serenity "in the banquet, the song and the harp, friendship, warm baths, sleep and love."

11

Writing and Publication

PART ONE

I'm not sure at what age I decided that I wanted to become a writer. As a child I wasn't a particularly zealous reader. For a time in the mid-1930s I became engrossed in reading the pulp magazines, among them *Tarzan, Guard of the Jungle, Ghost Stories*, and *The Spider*. The pulp I found most fascinating was *G8 and His Battle Aces*, containing stories of the World War I pilots who fought in their Spads and Sopwith Camel biplanes against the Fokkers of the German Air Force. In these stories British and American pilots were pitted in single combat against German pilots. The most famous German ace among these "Huns" was Baron Manfred von Richthofen, the "Red Baron" who foraged the skies in his distinctive scarlet Albatross triplane and who achieved 80 credited kills of Allied fighter pilots before he was shot down himself.

Unlike war in the trenches with men on both the Allied and German sides dying in senseless assaults back and forth across No Man's Land, the fighting in the air pitted identifiable heroes in valorous single combat. The triumphant pilots achieved fame and an identity we could read about as we admired their exploits.

What appealed to me was the element of gallantry in these air battles, absent in the fighting on the ground. After a dogfight, there was the dipping of plane wings to defeated flyers, and often the scattering of flowers over the crash site of fallen planes. The squadron of the English Air Force, one of whose pilots, Captain Brown had shot down

Richthofen on March 21, 1918, buried their famous adversary with full military honors including dropping a wreath on his grave reading "For a Worthy and Honorable Foe."

During my illness, I was again drawn to World War I while reading the poetry of Alan Seeger including his prophetic poem, "Rendez-vous with Death." On the eve of the infamous Battle of the Somme in 1916 where 25,000 men lost their lives in the first day of fighting, Seeger wrote:

> I have a rendezvous with Death
> At some disputed barricade,
> When Spring comes back with
> Rustling shade
> And apple-blossoms fill the air—
> I have a rendezvous with Death
> When Spring brings back blue
> days and fair.

I memorized that poignant poem and recited it over and over again, identifying with the pathos of the young soldiers dying in war.

I was also moved by the poetry of another World War I poet, Wilfred Owen, who, as with Seeger, was killed in the Great War. His poetry captured the disillusionment of young men going off to war prompted by high ideals only to lose them in the harsh brutality of the conflict. In Owen's poem "Disabled," a soldier whose legs have been amputated reflects on the reasons for his enlistment.

> It was after football, when he'd drunk a peg
> He thought he'd better join. He wonders why
> Someone said he'd look a god in kilts.
> That's why, and maybe, too, to please his Meg.

In this period I also read the shattering novel *All Quiet on the Western Front* by the German novelist Erich Maria Remarque. That book moved me to reject the validity of any war no matter the fervor of patriotic slogans that might prompt one to join.

I think those two years of illness with tuberculosis when I became an avid reader, more than anything else turned me to the creation of stories. Long before the era of television with the more appealing radio programs not broadcast until evening, my pastime became obsessively reading. Confined to bed, both day and night, with nothing else to do, I consumed one book after another.

In an effort to escape the confinement of my room, my imagination also flourished, allowing me to carry out make-believe journeys across the world that my illness prevented me from undertaking. Perhaps a fear of death that came frequently to my mind also fostered an urge in me to extricate some meaning in what I was feeling and fearing. I believe that preoccupation with illness and death helped nurture a tragic sense that from the beginning has been imbued in my work.

After I had been liberated from bed and returned to school as an adolescent, my first efforts at writing were in poetry. I recall an early (thankfully lost) poem titled "Ephemeral Splendor," which spoke of my love for some nymph I identified only by describing certain of her enticing body parts. Perhaps the reason I remember this otherwise forgettable verse was the controversy it created when it was published in our four-page mimeographed church newsletter.

The righteous president of our parish board was outraged and carried the mimeographed poem angrily to my father, warning him to reign in his blasphemous son before I blossomed into full perversity. He also suggested that some grueling and steady work be found for me in a grocery or restaurant to save me from these cesspools of depravity I was inhabiting.

My father mentioned the incident to me as a cautionary tale but I don't recall him being incensed or disturbed. I know that he felt some pride in my early efforts to write when his church secretary, a bright and devoted lady named Bessie Spirides told me that when my father had visitors he pulled from his desk drawer one of my early stories and showed it to his visitors saying, "My son wrote this. He's going to be a fine writer someday."

I cannot believe that my father saw any quality in what I had written at that time to warrant such a prediction. His own lack of fluency in English made him a poor judge of literature. Yet he could speak with faith about me based simply on his love for his youngest son.

In my adolescence I remember the titles of a few stories I wrote but only fragments of their substance. There was a story called "The Ballad of Billy One-Eye," the tale of an old sailor who had sailed the seven seas and had lost one eye in a fight over a woman. In a story called "Suella," a convict newly released from prison travels by train to a small town in the South to kill Suella, the woman who had betrayed him and caused him to be sent to prison. Another story titled "Ashes of the Rose" had as a principal character a man who had witnessed the death by fire of a schoolhouse full of children and who was tormented by the memory. Looking back it seems to me that those early stories often reflected a preoccupation with violence, passion and death.

My efforts at writing were desultory, at best. I'd feel the urge to write a story and after writing a few pages, put it aside. I rarely bothered to revise. Several months passed before I might feel the urge to write again.

I think my desire to pursue writing as a way of life was crystallized by an event that took place one winter when I was taking classes at Columbia College in Chicago. Still seeking some occupation to help support my family, I enrolled in a class on broadcasting. I had been told I had a good voice and broadcasting seemed a legitimate avenue to explore.

One of our class assignments that winter was to write a 300 to 400 word short story centered on Christmas. Afterwards, students were selected to read their stories for the class to discuss.

My story concerned a waiter who, returning home from work on Christmas Eve, finds his wife absent from their apartment. This wasn't the first time she was gone and he knew where he would find her. He walked to the neighborhood bar she frequented and found her drinking with several men. He took her home and, in a fit of frustration and anger, slapped her.

Remorseful at having struck her, he washed her face and helped put her to bed. Then he began decorating the small tree he had brought home in preparation for Christmas morning. He was consoled for a little while knowing that when his wife woke sober the next day, they'd share a few tranquil hours around the Christmas tree.

The reading of each story was followed by a spirited class discussion. None of my classmates showed any restraint in soundly thrashing a story they didn't like and I felt some apprehension about reading mine. After joining the discussion on several other stories, I decided a little warily to raise my hand and was selected to read my story.

At the conclusion of my reading my page-and-a-half story, which took no more than four to five minutes, I was met with absolute silence. My first bewildering thought was that the silence signified unanimous disapproval.

I stood there in anguish as the teacher pressed the class for comment. Finally, one student spoke up, confessing that he had little he wanted to say in the face of such a poignant personal experience.

That my story had to be true was the general reaction of the class. I was astonished because the story was a total fiction and I tried to assure the class of that fact. But they simply would not be convinced that I wasn't the young waiter suffering with an alcoholic wife.

After class I remember walking alone in the snow through Grant Park, the flakes falling in little icy pinpoints on my forehead and cheeks. I felt suddenly aware of a power in me I hadn't recognized before. If I could create characters that my listeners believed were real, perhaps I had talent as a writer that I needed to nurture.

DURING THIS TIME Diana, sweetheart of my adolescence, whom I had courted for several years, and I were married. After spending a few months living with my parents, we moved into a small third-floor studio apartment in the Kenwood neighborhood south of Hyde Park. The apartment was part of a courtyard complex containing several hundred apartments. In summer when the windows were open, the babble of a dozen foreign tongues and the aromas of assorted cuisines swirled through the air.

We became friendly with our neighbors whose doors were usually open to gain those currents of air we sorely needed. While we lived in this small apartment, our first son Mark was born in the same Woodlawn Hospital where three years later my father would die.

For a time I worked at the South Works of U.S. Steel in South Chicago on rotating shifts, eight to four, four to twelve and twelve to eight. On those night shifts I worked which brought me home exhausted in the morning, my wife would place our son in a buggy and walk him for hours so I might sleep. She'd push him along 47th Street East to the park and to her father's cleaning and repair shop on 53rd Street. Some of our son's earliest memories were of that store with its pungent odors of leather and cleaning fluids.

I don't recall writing during this period. The irregular hours of work at the mills made any writing schedule almost impossible. There was also the constricting confinement of the studio apartment, allowing for little privacy.

About this time we made a decision to buy a home with my parents. A sturdy, commodious brick house was found in South Shore, which we bought for $17,000. Although my father listed us as co-owners, I contributed nothing to the cost of the house. The $5000 down payment we used came from U.S. Savings Bonds my father had purchased during the war and which comprised the totality of his savings.

By this time I had left the steel mills and begun working for the Simoniz Company in Chicago, answering complaint letters from customers who used the company's furniture polish and automotive wax.

Sometimes in the evening when a certain restlessness possessed me, I retreated into one of the rooms of the house and sitting down at my typewriter, I worked on a story. I also made some desultory efforts to mail the manuscripts to a magazine. Few of these early artless manuscripts survive.

For a long time I received only printed rejection slips on the manuscripts I sent out. One such rejection from *Harper's Magazine* I remember to this day:

"We are forced for reasons of the limitations of space to reject many manuscripts, which are otherwise ably written and publishable."

AFTER A SPAN of about a year in which I received a half dozen of these printed rejections from *Harpers Magazine* attached to my stories, one came in the mail with a tiny alteration. Some unknown (and compassionate) hand had underlined in red ink the last line in the rejection slip, which read "ably written and publishable."

I find it hard to recap my exultation at that sign, tiny as it might have been, of a human and empathetic heart. I folded that rejection slip carefully and slipped it into my wallet. I carried and with scant urging, pulled out the fading slip for months, watching it becoming dog-eared and worn. When I was asked, "How's the writing going?" I'd whip out the rejection slip with its red underlining of the four words as proof of my progress.

My employment record continued to be erratic. After I had been fired from Simoniz for reasons which included insolence toward my superiors, I spent a year operating a shabby lunchroom named Arts Lunch, a monstrous experience that deserves and receives a chapter of its own in this book. Afterwards I returned to the steel mills for a second period of employment. That was followed by a few months as a helper on a Budweiser beer truck. I also put in a year working behind the counter in a garage, selling automotive parts. All this time, working in spurts, I continued to write and send off my stories.

These submissions were costly. Postage was required for the outside of the envelope and an equal amount of postage for the return envelope. Then, one often waited months for a manuscript to be returned with the ubiquitous printed rejection slips.

There were also assorted indignities. On a number of occasions, my envelope bearing first-class stamps had been replaced with one bearing third-class stamps. I was outraged at those thieves and imagined the wealth they acquired peeling off thousands of first-class stamps.

Sometimes the manuscripts had been carelessly handled and required retyping before I could send them out again. The front page of one of my stories came back with great brown coffee stains on the front page as if some editor had been using it as a coffee mat.

One story that had been sequestered with a literary magazine for almost a year was finally returned with a brief note of apology from the editor explaining that he'd been recalled to service in the Navy and had just been discharged. Once again I was indignant. While that patriotic lout was serving his country, my manuscript was languishing in his office.

After a while there were also a few encouraging notes, sometimes no more than a few scrawled words of praise in the margins of a rejection slip. "Good job . . . try us again." "Read Irwin Shaw's short stories . . ." A few editors also offered suggestions on ways to revise the story. After I'd revised and submitted it again, once more the stories were rejected.

I was grateful for each of these brief personal responses confirming the stories had been read. Though they are long departed from the earth, I still cherish Esther Shiverick and Edward Weeks at the *Atlantic*; Dudley Strassburg at *World Publishing*; George Wiswell at *Esquire*;

Eleanor Rawson at *Colliers*; Pat Papangelis at *Playboy*. Their brief notes of encouragement and praise nurtured me and kept me writing.

I was also greatly helped by a lady who became a dear friend as well as a mentor. Marjorie Peters was a former journalist, writer-teacher I had met through a friend. He took me the Parkway Community house where Marjorie conducted a writing workshop. In her well-attended workshop I first met Gwendolyn Brooks and her husband Henry Blakely, Lerone Bennett, Edward Peeks, Millen Brand, and other talented writer-poets.

When Marjorie began conducting a writing workshop in her Hyde Park home, I attended those sessions, as well.

But Marjorie's kindness and generosity to me went beyond the classroom. Seeing some vestiges of talent in my work she undertook to tutor me.

I can remember winter evenings while we lived in the small studio apartment in Kenwood when, after dinner, I would walk the snow-crusted streets to Marjorie's home. The two of us perched on a large pillow-strewn couch, a space heater glowing at our feet for warmth, Marjorie patiently and skillfully critiqued my stories. For all she did for me I owe her a massive debt of gratitude.

Marjorie also invited our family for holiday celebrations with her family, her psychologist husband Philip Bauer, her sister Pauline who was a nurse, and her talented pianist-composer son Pierre Long. I remember the warmth of those holiday gatherings that often included other friends. I also vividly remember from those years a Christmas tree Marjorie and her family had suspended from the ceiling.

IN 1953, while I was still working at Simoniz, I returned home one evening to find our dining-room table set with candles and wine glasses. The occasion, which my wife felt worth celebrating, was a letter from Edward Weeks, the distinguished editor of the *Atlantic* writing about my short story, "The Old Man." Weeks wrote that the editors admired my story although they could not agree that it was totally successful. They had been noting the improvement in my work and were impressed with my progress. He ended his letter by saying that he believed the *Atlantic* would soon be accepting one of my stories.

My wife and I toasted one another jubilantly that evening, I for my writing skill and she for her love and support, both of us anticipating that within a few weeks or at the most, a few months, I'd achieve publication. That milestone actually took three more years.

I'm not quite sure just when I began writing my first novel. I had a title, *Cry the Black Tears*, long before I put the first words on paper. The writing of the book took me a period of about six months, each day's pages triple-hole punched and inserted in a loose-leaf binder. As the writing magazines advised, I submitted an outline and a pair of sample chapters to a few book publishers.

In the months following that submission I received printed rejections from three or four publishers, return of the manuscript in my stamped envelope without any comment, and one handwritten, "Sorry." None of them commented on the book, or provided me any advice I might have found useful.

One of the editors I had been corresponding with was Dudley Strassburg who worked for a vanity publisher where a writer would pay to have his work self-published. I considered that possibility for a while and then discarded the idea of self-publishing.

When Dudley Strassburg moved to *World Publishing*, a regular trade publisher, we continued our correspondence. I wrote asking Dudley to provide me an impartial assessment on *Cry the Black Tears*.

He agreed and I sent him the manuscript in November of that year. Several weeks passed and then a couple of months. I jotted him a short note asking about the book. He answered saying he was extremely busy but would get to it as soon as he could. That was in the late winter and at the end of summer, almost a year after my original submission, his letter finally came.

Somewhere in my overflowing files and voluminous folders resides his three-page single-spaced letter. It is a masterpiece of critical analysis, which, at the time, struck me with the impact of a bat lashed across my head. If I could locate the letter I'd print it here in its searing entirety.

Dudley had long delayed responding because he didn't quite know how I'd react to the criticism. That was the preamble. Then he launched into me with the fervor of an assassin.

My writing was phony, pretentious, clumsy, overheated, an appalling regurgitation of Greek tragedy. My grammar was abominable, my spelling faulty, my use of words inaccurate. He mentioned the ellipses . . . , which he called a useful symbol in any piece of writing. In my case, he wrote, it was as if I had loaded a shotgun with ellipses and then aimed it at my manuscript, closed my eyes, and fired both barrels through the stack of pages.

As I read and reread the letter in shock and pain, I felt a shame and mortification that I had never felt in my life before. That was followed by a feeling of outrage wherein I wished the plagues of Pharaoh be lavished on that abominable editor! How dare the bloody twit skewer my pride in so destructive a way!

Then, as I read the letter for the ninth or tenth time, I began to comprehend what an invaluable critique I had received. I thought of all the publishers who returned my manuscript with only a printed rejection slip, not bothering to comment, allowing me to languish in my self-deception. Here was a respected and astute editor who was going to the effort of telling me what was wrong with my work.

I wrote Strassburg within a day, thanking him for his time and effort, and vowing I would strive to benefit by his criticism. Indeed there had already been improvement in my short stories since the novel had been written three years earlier. I had begun a second novel I had titled *Lion at My Heart*. I had two chapters written when I received the Strassburg letter.

I dumped the disgraced *Cry the Black Tears* in the back of a closet and returned to working on the new novel, taking care to implement the suggestions in Strassburg's letter. This effort wasn't without setbacks. I literally had to reeducate myself in rudiments of grammar, begin to revise more frequently and with greater care.

I found it hard to mark the milestones by which my work improved. I don't think there was any sudden leap of ability between the writing of one story and the next, but a gradual refinement in my understanding of how stories should be written. As I studied the work of other writers I noted time and time again how they achieved greater impact in simpler ways. Meanwhile, the very act of more frequent writing and rewriting helped tutor me in using language and creating scenes.

I understood that while it was acceptable to read and appreciate other writers, one had to exercise caution not to be unduly influenced by them. One writer I greatly admired was the gargantuan novelist, Thomas Wolfe. His cycle of novels beginning with *Look Homeward Angel*, were masterpieces I sought to emulate. Without Wolfe's genius, however, my replication of his plethora of adjectives produced cluttered and overheated passages of prose.

What became apparent to me was the importance of revision. My stories improved in relation to the number of times I reworked them. Three drafts proved better than two and four drafts proved better than three. As I became more intensely involved with the writing of stories, I found myself revising beginnings and endings and certain crucial scenes as many as eight to ten times.

These revisions were not drafts comprising full pages of manuscript. Working as I was then on a manual and, afterwards, an electric typewriter, if the first paragraph I had typed needed reworking I would remove the page, red-pencil my changes, and then insert a blank page to begin the page again.

I would use different color bond for the different drafts, stacking the discarded pages on my desk. When some friend ascended the steps to my study, I made sure they observed the imposing stacks of rainbow colored bond on my desk as proof of my craftsmanship.

In December of 1956, I was working as a real estate salesman for Baird & Warner in Hyde Park. My father had been dead for five years and my mother was living with us in the house we had bought with our parents on Ridgeland Ave. I wasn't selling houses very successfully and since my salary was based on commission, my family faced a lean Christmas. We had bought our sons a few pieces of clothing but, in lieu of any toys, I had purchased a small dog for six dollars I planned to give them as a joint gift.

All the stories I had been submitting had been returned with the exception of one, "Pericles on 31st Street," which I had sent in September to the *Atlantic*.

I had learned though experience not to allow the length of time a magazine held a story as any indication that it might be read or accepted. Magazines were notoriously slow in responding. But my experience with the *Atlantic* had returned my stories within a couple of weeks. Each one also came with a brief note, sometimes from Edward Weeks, or from another fine *Atlantic* editor, Esther Shiverick.

Apprehensive that editors would not look favorably on Christmas telegrams from impatient writers, I still mustered the bravado to send a telegram to Edward Weeks at the *Atlantic*. I asked him simply for confirmation that my story hadn't been lost. I didn't dare ask him whether it was being considered.

That telegram was sent four days before Christmas and two days later, returning to the real estate office, I found a return telegram on my desk. Fearing some harsh condemnation for my rash inquiry I opened it.

"We are buying your story 'Pericles on 31st Street' as an *Atlantic First*. Congratulations and Merry Christmas. Edward Weeks."

I must have read those few words at least a score of times, each time savoring and feasting on them.

I surely conveyed the news to my associates in the office, but I have no memory of doing so. All my energy was focused on getting home to carry the joyful tidings to my family.

In the house, I read the telegram to Diana and to my mother. Diana hugged me with tears in her eyes and my mother made her cross in thanks to God. It was a fleeting but still grand moment of restitution for all the announcements of firings and small misfortunes I had brought home to them before.

I had an appointment later that afternoon at the real estate office so I drove back to Hyde Park. On the way I stopped to visit the venerable Rockefeller Chapel on the University of Chicago campus. From time to time in the past, during a fretful day, I would enter the chapel to sit for a while in that serene environment. On several occasions I had been fortunate to catch an organist or a choir practicing, the music enhanced in that spacious interior.

That afternoon the great chapel was empty of any other human. I sat in one of the rear pews and, after a few moments in the silence, I began to cry. My tears erupted from a surfeit of emotion that had finally found an outlet.

I cried with a joy born of ten years of futility. I cried for my father, dead five years, whose love saw my future. I cried for the hardships

Diana had endured and for her patience and devotion. I cried to release the torrents of joy surging through my heart.

I wasn't a total fool and understood that the sale of a single story was only a rudimentary step into the world of publishing, that the road ahead would be a difficult and continuing struggle. But the acceptance of my first story by a prestigious magazine after what had seemed an eternity of effort was a fulfillment I felt I deserved to savor.

Writing and Publication

PART TWO

In the months that followed the sale of "Pericles on 31st Street," there were several additional sales. The *Atlantic* bought a second story, "The Courtship of the Blue Widow"; the *Saturday Evening Post* bought "The Wooing of Ariadne."

At the end of that year another surprise came from the *Atlantic*. Among the half dozen *Atlantic Firsts* by new authors they had published that year, "Pericles on 31st Street" had been awarded first prize. On top of the initial $400 stipend I had received for the sale of the story, I was sent an additional $750. Not a large sum of money but to me at the time comprising the treasury of Croesus.

While writing short stories I had also been working on *Lion at My Heart,* the novel I began after discarding the soundly trashed *Cry the Black Tears.* I had written about four chapters or sixty pages and had sent that block of material to an agent I had acquired in New York named Toni Strassman.

I had queried Toni Strassman after asking both Edward Weeks at the *Atlantic* and George Wiswell at *Esquire* for the names of agents they had worked with and trusted. Toni Strassman's name was on both their lists.

Toni ran a one-woman agency in New York but brought to her work a wealth of literary experience. For years she had been a senior editor at Viking Press where she had worked as an editor for John Steinbeck.

I wrote Toni about taking me on as a client. She agreed to look at my work and, after reading a half dozen of my stories, agreed to represent me. Along with a couple of new short stories, I sent her the first chapters of *Lion at My Heart*.

Meanwhile, the sale of a few stories did little to alleviate our family economic problems. Something drastic had to be done about my finding steady employment. In an effort to help us, my brother Dan, a Service Manager for U.S. Steel obtained an interview for me as a speechwriter in the company headquarters in Pittsburgh. U.S. Steel paid for my airline ticket from Chicago to Pittsburgh and I arranged a stopover in New York so I could meet my new agent.

Toni Stresemann was a small, gracious lady, fine-featured with an engaging smile. She told me that she had arranged a meeting for me to meet the editors at Viking Press. After lunch we went to the Viking offices.

A secretary led us into the office of the publisher, Marshal Best, a handsome man of middle age who greeted us cordially. We were joined a few moments later by the senior editor at Viking, Pascal Covici, a man with a weathered but smile-warmed face and a great mane of white hair.

Before our visit Toni had told me a little about both men, who were giants in publishing. Marshall Best had led Viking to a position of great prestige in the industry. Covici had owned his own press, and then moved to Viking where he brought with him, John Steinbeck. While at Viking, he also worked as an editor with Arthur Miller, Joseph Campbell, and Shirley Jackson. A measure of the esteem with which Covici was regarded as an editor and friend to writers was that Saul Bellow's novel *Herzog,* John Steinbeck's *East of Eden* and Shirley Jackson's *We Have Always Lived in the Castle* were all dedicated to Covici.

What Toni had not told me was that she had sent the first chapters of my novel *Lion at My Heart* to Viking. Both men had read the chapters, admired the work, and were eager to see the remainder of the book. Most amazingly, that day in their office they offered me a contract.

I sat there swept by a multitude of emotions, first shock and disbelief and then delight. Toni sat beaming and, after I had signed a contract and been given a check for $1500, we left the Viking offices.

We were joined by another friend of Toni she wished me to meet, a lovely Greek lady named Vasiliki Sarant who until his death had been married to the brilliant novelist, Isaac Rosenfeld. To celebrate the new contract, the two ladies took me to a penthouse cocktail lounge with a terrace overlooking the New York skyline. I had a margarita, a second and then a third. These had little additional effect because I was already drunk on the nectar of jubilation.

We stood on the penthouse terrace under a balmy night and starry sky. Vasiliki and Toni went inside and I lingered for a few moments alone on the terrace looking across the illuminated city of New York.

I cannot recall whether I cried out the words or merely thought them, words borrowed blatantly from the great novels and passion of Thomas Wolfe . . . "I'll bring you to your knees, bitch Goddess!"

I never achieved that auspicious goal but, at this stage of my life, that achievement doesn't seem to matter.

Later that evening, bountiful contract and cherished check in my pocket, I returned to my hotel, which bordered Central Park. The windows were open and I could hear the clomping of the horse carriages carrying sightseers through the park. The night was fragrant with the scent of myriad flowers.

I had phoned Diana earlier to tell her the news and I phoned her again. We spoke for a long while. Afterwards, excitement preventing me from sleeping, my thoughts roamed across the past and foraged into the future. I felt pride and power as if they were infusions of blood seeping into my body. In my delirium, I felt myself entering the hallowed legion of Melville and Tolstoy, Hawthorne and Hemingway.

THE FOLLOWING DAY I flew from New York to Pittsburgh. After interviewing in the U.S. Steel offices, I was hired as a speechwriter for junior-level executives. That was a job I intensely disliked and held for no more than about a year.

Two major events took place while we lived in Pittsburgh. That was the birth of our third son, Dean, and the publication of my first novel, *Lion at My Heart*. In the end, the book wasn't published by Viking Press, which, despite their initial enthusiasm, had decided against publication, but by the Atlantic Monthly Press under the editorial guidance of Edward Weeks.

For the year we spent in Pittsburgh, we lived in a suburb of the city called Whitehall, along a rural street called Provost Road. Behind the house we had rented was a great valley filled with thickly foliaged trees. At various seasons of the year, thousands of birds nested for a while in that forest and then scattered into the air in flocks so thick they blocked out the sun and darkened the sky.

While we lived in the suburb of Whitehall, the doctor and hospital we would use for the birth of our third child was in Mt. Lebanon, some considerable distance away. To make sure I wouldn't get lost if Diana went into labor at night, I drove the route several times.

The night Diana went into labor and I bundled her into my car, I drove off grateful for my having tracked the route. But ten minutes from our house I ran into a detour that thwarted all my well-laid plans. After a desperate half hour driving the dark roads, I found my way to the hospital. Diana was admitted and I entered the waiting area.

After a short while a nurse appeared to tell me that Diana was hours away from any birth and that I might go home and return later. I said goodbye to my wife, and drove home. As I entered our house, the phone rang. The call was from the hospital informing me that our third son had been born.

I showered and rushed back to the hospital to see Diana. She looked exhausted but very beautiful. As I embraced her, she scolded me for wearing one of the washed and pressed shirts she had prepared for me to use for work while she was confined.

When we saw our new son for the first time, he was as handsome as all newborn babies are in the loving eyes of their parents.

The other event that took place during our sojourn in Pittsburgh was the arrival of the first copy of my book. I had been through the preliminary stages, correcting the manuscript in galleys and returning them to the publisher. I was told a few months would be required to complete the process. As the months passed I began waiting impatiently for each day's mail.

I'm not sure what month it was but the book arrived on a Saturday. I recall that because our sons were home and not in school. I was in an upstairs bedroom and from the window I saw the mail truck pull up to our rural mailbox. I caught a tantalizing glimpse of a small brown package the mailman slipped into our box. I rushed down-stairs, shouting to my family as I passed, "It's here!"

I retrieved the package from my publisher and carried it into the house. Opening it I pulled out the virgin copy of my first published book.

I had always loved the aroma of books—that confluence of ink and paper that marked a new book before human hands wore it down. I had smelled books in libraries before but I swore that day inhaling the scent from my own book brought a new, more fragrant aroma into my nostrils.

I leafed through the pages, stroked the jacket, and admired the photograph of myself on the rear of the jacket. All this time my family was rejoicing as I rejoiced. All our shouting wakened the baby and he began to cry. Diana picked Dean up to console him.

In a celebratory procession we marched around the house. Our two older sons led the family, holding pots and large metal spoons, which they banged on the bottom of the pots to raise a deafening clamor. Diana followed behind them holding the baby. I trailed the procession, holding the book in both hands above my head, as a priest in church might hold aloft the chalice of communion.

Despite my abhorrence of the speechwriting job, there was a certain serenity to our surroundings. In front of our house, on a hill overlooking Provost Road, was an old Civil War cemetery. With Dean in his buggy and our older sons walking alongside, Diana and I would walk the path winding among the tombstones.

We also played games in the terrain along the back of our house, a thick grove of trees ideal for games of hide-go-seek.

But I grew more and more restless. I thoroughly detested the job, which involved writing speeches for junior level executives. The process generally included a preliminary meeting with half a dozen or more company men and women, each one contributing what they felt the message of the speech should contain. Since it was impossible to please them all, I wrote speeches that pleased no one. The only reason I wasn't fired earlier was the company connection to my brother.

I went to work each day, riddled with frustration, longing to begin my life as a freelancer. The sale of a few stories and a first novel hardly justified so reckless a move. Everyone with any knowledge of the writing field, Marshall Best, Pascal Covici, Toni Strassman, all warned me against such a foolhardy decision. But I was like a crazed fox that had been given a scent of his prey and I was wild to join the chase.

One of the bounties of the Pittsburgh job was making friends with my fellow workers. An older writer in my department who mentored and befriended me was Herb Depew. Genial and soft-spoken, he sought to harness my impatience and curb my excesses.

"You don't have to love your job," Herb told me. "Just do it for those hours a day you need to work so you can support your family. Write your own stories after dinner and on weekends."

Another younger, zestful coworker who became a good friend was Ron Ridgeway who had been a fighter pilot in World War II. Ron, a handsome and ebullient man who was about my age, worked in sales. A bounty of his friendship, he assured me, would be his zealous assistance in the merchandising of my novel.

In the morning Ron and I would ride the Shannon Trolley from the suburb of Whitehall into downtown Pittsburgh to U.S. Steel headquarters. The trolley cars were always crowded and so we younger men generally stood for the journey holding to overhead straps. Ron held onto the strap with one hand while his other hand held an open copy of my novel, its bright orange jacket clearly revealing the book's title, *LION AT MY HEART*.

While the train rolled and rocked along the curving track, Ron kept up a loud chorus of superlatives.

"Wow! Great! What writing! What sex! What a plot!"

With another coworker named Pierce Platt who had published some stories and articles and who also aspired to freelance, we two writers spent hours discussing our future. He had three daughters and I had three sons and that seemed a fortuitous joining of families. Pierce also had a good friend in Mexico who provided us information on housing and English-speaking schools.

For a short while we considered moving with our families to Mexico. That move across the border never materialized but, finally, probably preempting my getting fired by only a few weeks, I quit my job.

Diana was apprehensive about our family's future, but manifesting an abundance of faith and love, went along with my decision. We packed up and returned to Chicago where I would begin my future life as a freelance writer. My family of brothers and sisters as well as a number of friends, thought me demented.

My reckless disregard of reality might surely have led to disaster had it had not been for the love and generosity of my nephews, Leo, Frank and Steve Manta, and their parents.

Their father, John Manta, owned a number of properties including an old house near the lake in South Shore. At the turn of the century the gable-roofed, three-story dwelling on East 75th Street had basked in a period of gaslight elegance but in the years that followed had fallen upon forlorn times. The house had been sold half a dozen times, and in more recent years was utilized as a boarding house before being abandoned and later condemned. John Manta had bought the house for the land and within a year planned for the old structure to be demolished.

My nephews prevailed upon their father to delay the demolition and allow my family to occupy the house. When he agreed, we faced the imposing task of making the house habitable. I joined my nephews in a rigorous effort at renovation. We washed the walls and then painted them with a thick textured paint to cover the numerous cracks. We sanded the floors, scavenged furniture and rugs from the houses of relatives, and using a time payment plan, bought several new kitchen appliances.

We were helped enormously by a few other relatives and some good friends who pitched in with their skill and their labor. My brother-in-law Ray Fox, an electrician by trade, rewired all the faulty lines. One of my closest and dearest friends was a debonair Irishman named Jack Murray. As youths we had spent hours together philosophizing about life and our ambitions. On my wedding day, since I had not yet learned to drive, Jack had driven me to the cleaners to pick up my dark suit and then drove me to the church for my wedding. Jack was one of those gifted individuals skilled in all trades from plumbing to carpentry to electricity. We would never have been able to inhabit the house except for his valorous assistance.

On a day when I was painting in the house with Steve, the youngest of my Manta nephews, the phone rang. The call was from New York, from my agent Toni Strassman, with the jubilant news that *Lion at My Heart* had been sold to the premiere television program on the air at that time, *Playhouse 90*. The prestigious producing/directing team of Ed Lewis and John Frankenheimer would make the film.

Playhouse 90 had produced in a live format, in one and a half hour programs, some of the most outstanding dramas on television. These included *Marty, Requiem for a Heavyweight* and *12 Angry Men* created by writers such as Rod Serling and Reginald Rose.

After receiving the call, Steve and I piled into the car to carry the news to Diana and our sons who were staying with John and Barbara Manta. My decision to freelance was given, for that moment at least, a shade more credence.

(The disappointment we would not learn about until a few months later, was that *Playhouse 90* would close down and cease producing plays before *Lion at My Heart* could be broadcast.)

But, at that time, the sale of *Lion at My Heart* to *Playhouse 90* seemed a beneficent talisman gracing our move into the renovated house. After our extensive labor, the old dwelling sparkled with a vestige of its former grandeur.

In that old house by the lake, I began my career as a free-lance writer. By adding teaching and lecturing, I established the life I have now lived for more than 50 years.

13

Lecturing, Teaching, and Storytelling

The somber truth is that without the supplemental income I earned from years of lecturing and, in addition, those interludes I spent teaching, I wouldn't have survived as a freelancer. My family would have faced economic calamity.

As a youth I had performed in school plays, mostly Greek tragedies in which I played the roles of both those haunted kings, Creon and Oedipus. I had no dramatic training but a strong voice, which I used flagrantly to compensate for my lack of acting skills. I did not perform my roles, as much as shout them, did not enthrall my audience as much as try to overpower them. Fortunately, my voice fitted the dramatic crescendos of Sophocles and Euripides.

The first public speaking I did took place years after those dramatic performances, in 1959 when I had gone to work for U.S. Steel in Pittsburgh. The occasion was a book review I did before the Sewickly Woman's Club, an affluent suburb of Pittsburgh. I had gotten to know Arthur Buckholz, the manager of the book department at Kauffman's Department Store in downtown Pittsburgh. I'd drop into the department during my lunch break, browse among the books, and chat with the literate Buckholz about books and writing.

Buckholz set up a modest promotional signing for my first novel, *Lion at My Heart*, an autographing sparsely attended by a few of my coworkers at U.S. Steel. As I autographed a copy for one of our company secretaries, she told me she was buying the book for her secretarial pool. When one girl finished reading the book, it would be passed on to another. She seemed delighted to be able to share that news, but all I could gloomily surmise was that twenty people were going to purchase a single copy.

As for the fate of the autographing, in addition to the secretary's copy, we sold two more copies, one of them bought by Buckholz for his own library.

One day Buckholz asked if I'd like to do a book review for a woman's club. He had been scheduled to do the review but had a conflict in dates. I needed only to read the book, and then report on it to the ladies of the club. My fee for the event would be $25.

I accepted, read the book and appeared before the Sewickley Woman's Club to report on the book. A few days later while receiving my check for $25 from Buckholz, I asked if he had heard any assessment of my performance.

"The program chairwoman said they would have preferred a little less about Petrakis and more about the book."

For about a year, I lectured under the direction of a national speaker's bureau named Colston-Leigh. When we moved from Pittsburgh back to Chicago, through the recommendation of the poet Gwendolyn Brooks who with her husband, Henry Blakely, had become treasured friends, I was introduced to Gwendolyn's lecture agent, Beryl Zitch of the Contemporary Forum.

Beryl was a small and vivacious woman, wonderfully animated in voice and gestures. She and her husband Gene Zitch also became good friends with whom we shared birthdays and holidays.

Beryl was a zealous and accomplished agent. She began actively pushing me for college and club engagements. Under Beryl's energetic direction, I not only began more frequent lecturing but also started receiving larger fees.

I sorely regret not having kept a journal or some kind of record of the several hundred lectures I did for Beryl through a ten-year period. In my faulty efforts at recall, one college, university and club blends into another. Certain details about these visits remain the same while a few experiences stand out.

One of my first lectures in Chicago was for a women's club and was made memorable by the collapse of a lady in my audience, who, while I was speaking, fell from her chair on the aisle onto the floor. The only other male present was the club caretaker and, while one of the ladies phoned 911, the caretaker and I carried the stricken lady to a couch.

I confess now that the old theater saying, "I knocked them dead," came to my mind. I wondered if anything I said had precipitated the lady's collapse. And, young and insensitive as I was then, I couldn't help wondering whether her death in the middle of my lecture would be an asset or a hindrance in my future bookings.

I would leave home for two to three weeks, to begin a road trip that would schedule me to speak before a university or a club audience at least every other day. Sometimes my speaking engagements were on successive days. I'd fly out of O'Hare or Midway airports in Chicago to a college and then follow an itinerary Beryl had set up. I'd speak by day and travel at night by bus, train or commuter airline to another college.

I'd arrive in a small college town in the evening and generally be picked up by an associate instructor in the English department. If my arrival was early enough we'd have dinner and then he'd drive me to my hotel or motel. From the lack of enthusiasm some of these instructors displayed as they looked after me, I suspected lots had been drawn and the loser sent to greet me.

In those days before the illuminated signs of Holiday Inn and Ramada became ubiquitous across the country's landscape, the hotels I stayed in all seemed to bear names like the sections of cemeteries, Sleepy Hollow and Shady Rest.

The lobbies of these shabby hostelries all smelled musty as mausoleums. Confirming that bleak impression, in a corner of the lobby, a local would be sprawled in an armchair, his eyes closed and his body motionless. I could never be sure whether the man was dozing or dead and had simply been forgotten.

For some reason the sharpest image I have of these hotels was a succession of hallways dimly lit with low wattage, unshielded bulbs, the wallpaper a nondescript pattern of faded flowers. The worn rug under my feet emanated the tread of the dejected and weary travelers who had walked those desolate corridors before me.

If it were summer, the room's creaky window air conditioner rattled and ran only intermittently. If I occupied these hotel rooms in winter, steam hissed and knocked in the rusted radiators. I would sleep that night on a mattress that smelled of futility and illicit love. In the morning I'd rise to shave before a vanity mirror that was always cracked. As I stared at my distorted visage in the cracked glass, I saw reflected back the forlorn faces of all those poor melancholy wretches who had stood in the dawn before that same mirror.

A different instructor or sometimes a professor would be waiting in the lobby and, after a cup of coffee and a muffin; we'd begin a day of visiting classes and speaking to students. This routine, as numerous poets and novelists traveling the lecture circuit would confirm, could be exhilarating and exhausting. Exhilarating because one has the opportunity to initiate a spirited dialogue that might prove of some value to the young men and women.

The process could be exhausting, as well, because of the vitality of the students, their eagerness to have answers about writing and life when no definite answers existed. Their hunger for explanations assaulted me like a virus sucking away my energy.

The problem was trying to convey to these young people lessons about writing and life that I myself was still learning. Even as I stood before them, posing as a paragon of wisdom and experience, how was I able to tell them that I was still immersed in an ongoing process of discovering who I was?

Those cross-country trips merge into a multitude of the faces and voices of young men and young women. Their teachers were generally accommodating, sometimes had even read one of my books in anticipation of my visit.

From time to time I would find one critical or resentful about my heralded one-day appearances. One blunt-tongued teacher at a college whose name I've forgotten referred to me as a "courtesan of literature."

"You come in for a single day, and speak several times," he told me. "You bask in the student's enthusiasm and applause. Then you leave and don't have to deal with the students, day after day, class after class, for months at a time until you're sick and weary of them and they've become sick and tired of you."

In this sequence of traveling and speaking, there were some memorable experiences. One such moment came at the end of a three-week period I had spent on the road. I was exhausted and anxious to get home but had one more school visit still before me.

From a college town in Nevada, I flew into the airport at Waco, Texas where I was scheduled to speak the following day to English students at Baylor University. I was already looking beyond that visit and, finally, being able to go home.

The night I flew into Waco, the weather was bleak, the plane ride rocky with a heavy rain pelting the windows. I sat nervous and brooding in the small commuter plane, wondering if there wasn't a less onerous way for me to earn a living. The plane landed at the Waco airport with a series of bumps as if the pilot were also at the end of his patience.

When I emerged from the small plane, and descended the steps, instead of being met by the customary English instructor, I was greeted by a delegation of a dozen students. One exceptionally lovely girl stepped forward to greet me. She had enticing blonde tresses, an exquisite face and great glowing eyes. She flashed me a warm, welcoming smile as she handed me a single full blooming white rose. With a rich southern drawl reminiscent of Scarlett O'Hara in *Gone with the Wind* she said, "Mr. Petraaaakisss, Baylor University welcomes you . . ."

In that sparkling, unexpected moment my weariness fled and I felt rejuvenated. However, that sparkling greeting is all I can remember of my visit to Baylor.

During another writers' conference at Indiana University, one of my fellow faculty members was a gracious man and a fine poet named Lionel Wiggam. He was also fortunate in being a handsome man with an actor's flair, whose readings of his poetry were moving and dramatic. Our hotel rooms were next to one another and, after a day of classes and conferences, sometimes joined by a few other writer\teachers, we had a few drinks.

Late one evening as I was returning to my room, I found a young, attractive girl curled up asleep on the floor outside my door. My initial feeling was a suffusion of gratitude at this demonstration of affection for me as teacher and perhaps, hopefully, as a man.

I reached down and shook her shoulder gently in an effort not to startle her. I was close enough to hear her, still half asleep, whisper the name "Lionel . . . Lionel . . ."

She had simply confused my room with that of the poet next door.

"Get up!" I said brusquely. "You can't sleep here! Get up!"

There was another night, in another year, when I flew in to address a convocation at a small Baptist college. I can no longer remember the college but the state, I think, might have been Louisiana.

For that visit I was picked up at the airport by the dean of the college, a gracious gentleman who was also an ordained Baptist minister. We drove through the dark countryside and spoke about the college, a small liberal arts school with an enrollment of about 800 students. When I asked how many students the dean anticipated would be present at the convocation the following morning, he replied that since attendance wasn't compulsory, based on past experience, he anticipated about thirty to forty.

I muttered something about that number being inadequate in relation to the school enrollment. We drove in silence for a few more miles through the darkness of the southern countryside and then the dean who was also an ordained minister spoke to me in a grave and reproving voice.

"Mr. Petrakis, the Master, Jesus Christ, spoke to only twelve."

Since that fateful night I have never dared to complain about any audience as long as there were at least twelve.

Before different lecture groups, I have repeated that story of the Baptist dean's rebuke many times. I told it once to a group at the Martin Luther King Library on Chicago's South Side. We were in the middle of winter and snow had been falling all day across the city. At twilight the streets were filled with great mounds of snow pushed toward the curbs by the plows.

A small group had assembled in an alcove of the library. Counting my wife Diana, six library patrons, three librarians and myself, there were eleven of us. Just as I finished wryly relating the story of the Baptist minister and how that night we had not made the quorum of twelve, the library door opened and a solitary woman, bundled in coat and scarf, emerged from the snow and wind to join us and make up the twelve.

Another experience came during a period in the early 1980s when I was suffering my suicidal depression. This visit to a college in Wisconsin was the fateful trip when I planned to phone Diana and tell her I was remaining in Wisconsin overnight. My intent was to fly into Chicago as scheduled, pick up my car at the airport, and drive to Indiana where I intended to end my life.

I spoke several times at the college that day, my presentations tinged with a melancholy that came because I felt these were among the last words I would be speaking. Later that day while having coffee with a group of teachers, a faculty member told me about another teacher who had been in the audience when I spoke.

"He has been sorely depressed for more than a year. He told me that after your talk, for the first time in a year, he could feel his depression lifting."

WHEN I APPEARED BEFORE AUDIENCES at colleges, churches, clubs and synagogues, there were always the introductions to be endured first. One could never anticipate the mess of inaccuracies those introductions might comprise. I was often credited with awards I had not received including, on several occasions, the Pulitzer and once, by an overzealous chairwoman, the Nobel Prize for Literature. I usually corrected these errors but if they were modest additions to my biography, I sometimes let them pass.

Among the introductions that I received on half a dozen occasions and vigorously corrected each time were those presenters who introduced me with fervor as, "Mr. Petrakis . . . the world-renowned author of *Zorba the Greek!*"

They had, of course, confused Harry Mark Petrakis with Nikos Kazantzakis, the great author not only of *Zorba* but of half a hundred other memorable books. Our most gratifying link was that the heritage of both of us stemmed from the majestic island of Crete.

The work of Kazantzakis had provided me insight into the soul of Greece and I revered him as the greatest of the modern Greeks.

One of the longest and most bewildering of these introductions was provided to me when I was to speak before a Greek Church somewhere in the East. The man chosen to introduce me was a World War II veteran, a member of the U. S. 27th Armored Infantry Battalion, a vital component of Operation Lumberjack, when on March 7, 1945, the battalion captured the Ludendorff Bridge at Remagen in Germany.

My introducer spoke for half an hour, paused to get his second wind, and then continued for another half hour. A word of praise for me was followed by several references to the history of the bridge whose original structure had been built by the Romans to accommodate the troops of Caesar. My introducer tracked the history of the bridge from ancient to modern times and, finally, delivered explicit details about its capture.

"I wish Mr. Petrakis had been with us on that fateful day so in his brilliant style he would be able to write of the dramatic capture of the Ludendorff Bridge at Remagen!"

He spoke passionately of the fierce fighting that preceded the bridge's capture, the daring exploits of the soldiers, and, in the end, the strategic importance of that first crossing of the Rhine River.

In my presenter's words, "the bridge was worth its weight in gold by opening that gateway for invasion by the armies of Generals Patton and Gen Bradley."

From time to time the introducer paused for breath and to allow time for the anticipated flurry of applause.

While I felt some historical interest in his story and admired the passion with which he delivered it, I had the uneasy feeling that all the enthusiasm and energy had been drained from my audience as we all relived the drama of the capture of the Ludendorff Bridge at Remagen.

The lectures were followed by the autographings. I would be seated at a table, smiling up at people, asking politely how the book should be signed and how the names were spelled. I tried to remain courteous and patient as a man or woman, with a line of men and women waiting behind them, lingered while eagerly relating to me their own life stories.

Sometimes they'd catch me in a corner and confess to a compulsion to write their stories. A man who had lost his wife after fifty years of marriage wished to immortalize his love for her in a book. He had never written a book before and asked me seriously, "How do I start?" A woman who had lost her child to leukemia wanted to write that mournful story. An older Greek man, speaking to me in a whisper, confessed that in his youth he had murdered a man in his village in Greece. He'd been haunted all his life by the crime and felt that by writing it down he'd exorcize his demons. I strongly urged him to forget the whole business.

As my work became better known, I was invited to participate as writer/teacher at writers' conferences held in the summer at various universities. I believe I was a helpful, empathetic teacher and on a number of occasions was asked to return. I taught five summers at Indiana University in Bloomington, Indiana, two of those years taking place in the 1960s when I taught with a young Kurt Vonnegut who wore his hair at that time in a crew cut. Five summers at Illinois Wesleyan University, four summers at the University of Rochester in New York, five summers at the University of Wisconsin School of the Arts in Rhinelander, Wisconsin.

I cannot begin to list the names of all those wonderful writer-teachers, novelists and poets, I taught alongside at these conferences. A few became good friends with whom I maintained correspondence for years.

For two years in the late 1970s, I served as writer-in-residence for the Chicago Public Library under a program titled Writing-Out-Loud sponsored by a grant from the National Division of the Humanities. The program was directed by an engaging young librarian named Stephen Kochoff.

During those two years I visited twenty-seven city libraries, doing one-day workshops or setting up writing seminars that met once a week for a four-week total. These seminars brought me into contact with aspiring writers from across the city.

What the workshops revealed to me was the hunger for expression that existed within people in all walks of life. One of my larger classes comprising about 75 students at the Edgewater Library had in it a dentist, a cardiologist, two policemen, a physical therapist, a nurse, a pharmacist and a dozen representatives of still other professions.

THE TWO YEARS I SPENT writer-in-residence with the Chicago Public Library were followed by two years as writer-in-residence with the Chicago Board of Education. In those two years I visited sixty-three elementary, middle school, and high schools, conducting seminars on writing and storytelling.

I visited blighted areas of Chicago I never knew existed, shabby storefront schoolrooms in century-old buildings to state-of-the-art classrooms in sparkling modern structures.

One of the school experiences that remain vivid for me to this day was my visit to the Jenner Elementary School under the shadow of the Cabrini-Green housing developments, one of the poorest areas of the city.

The principal, Mr. Cox, greeted me as I entered the school and took diligent care of me through what was an extraordinary day.

The young students at Jenner were dressed in their Sunday clothing, and following my presentation, they performed a stunning presentation of their own, reading short essays and poems they had written in preparation for my visit. The day for me was profoundly moving.

On two occasions I served yearlong teaching assignments. In the mid-1970s, I held the McGuffey Visiting Lectureship at Ohio University in Athens, Ohio. In 1992 I held the Nikos Kazantzakis Chair in Modern Greek Studies at San Francisco State University.

Both these years of teaching and meeting with students were arduous and yet rewarding and stimulating because of the classroom exchanges with students and the opportunity of meeting other faculty members. Both assignments helped me understand and admire the rigors required to teach. With a minimal teaching load, between classroom lectures and then meeting with students, by the end of the day I would be exhausted. If I'd had to endure a full workload of teaching, I didn't see how I could have any energy remaining to write. But a number of the professors on the faculty of both Ohio University and San Francisco State University, in addition to their full teaching loads, had also written and published books.

Ohio University at the time I was teaching had a group of writing stars on its faculty. These included Walter Tevis who had written *The Hustler*, Daniel Keyes, the author of *Flowers for Algernon* that became the movie *Charley*. There was also the wonderful poet, Hollis Summers and the English professor and Spanish War veteran, James

Norman Schmidt, and the professor and essayist, Edward Quattrocchi. All of these writers with whom I taught became friends. In addition on a number of evenings we played some spirited games of poker together.

San Francisco State was also an enriching experience that allowed Diana and myself to live a memorable year in that cosmopolitan city by the bay. With the guidance and assistance of the professor, poet and director of the Modern Greek Studies program, Prof. Thanasis Maskalares, my classes were established.

San Francisco State was a vigorous learning institution, its students active and vocal. During the period of the Vietnam War, along with the campuses of Berkeley, California and Ball State in Ohio, the student body provided some of the most vociferous protests of any university in the country.

San Francisco State was at the opposite end of the spectrum from the haughty quadrangles of Harvard and Yale, a rough-hewn emporium of education, with a relatively small campus to accommodate a student enrollment of about 28,000. As a consequence of this limited space, there were crowds everywhere, in the corridors of buildings, in the libraries and on the walks. With the sun shining, literally thousands of students reclined singly or in groups on the expanse of grass.

The campus was also a thriving bazaar. There were booths and tables staffed by students who sold an assortment of scarves, t-shirts, watches, brief cases, costume jewelry and other assorted products. That kind of massive flea market I had never seen at any other school anywhere else in the country.

Along with the selling of assorted items there was dialogue, often becoming vociferous and passionate. There were groups arguing religion or politics, collecting signatures and donations to support assorted causes, from nuclear disarmament to global warming.

Those years I traveled back and forth across the country so many times, the hundreds of clubs, churches and colleges I visited, provided our family income we needed on which to live. But those years were also valuable for me as I absorbed the voices and opinions of hundreds of students and teachers, listened to them speak of their dreams and longings as well as their disappointments and their despair.

At this stage of my life, looking back across those years, I am amazed at the multitudinous times I lectured and the many classes I taught. I can only hope that the whirlwind of words that emerged from my lips might have, here and there, provided at least a modest measure of insight and value for some of those young men and young women who heard me.

14

Hollywood

PART ONE

My first year as a freelance writer netted our family of five about $1600. My second year saw that paltry sum increased to a still meager $2400. We survived on the generosity of relatives and friends who invited us to lunches and dinners. We ate several times a week with Diana's parents, her mother filling my plate while also serving me a generous portion of the evil eye. An uneasy thought crossed my mind that in her culinary preparation, replicating the Borgias, she might decide to rid the world of her shiftless son-in-law.

David McKay had published my novel *The Odyssey of Kostas Volakis* in 1963. In 1965 I published my first short story collection, *Pericles on 31st Street* with Quadrangle Books, a small Chicago publisher. Several New York publishers had turned the collection down, telling me that short stories don't sell.

Quadrangle was owned by a pair of publishing entrepreneurs, Mel Brisk and Ivan Dee. They gambled in bringing out a book of short stories by a little-known author. After the book was published, they were rewarded for their valor by having the collection nominated for the National Book Award in Fiction.

The day they heard the news of the nomination, Mel phoned Diana and she phoned the college where I was teaching a daylong writing workshop. A secretary brought me the news, which I excitedly announced to my class. Trying to maintain a demeanor of modesty, I basked in their resounding applause.

I drove from the school to the *Quadrangle* offices where Mel and Ivan had brought in several bottles of champagne. Diana had caught a train to downtown Chicago and joined us. We drank several glasses of champagne apiece and toasted the sagacity of the National Book Award judges, the literary acumen of the publishers and the extraordinary talent of the writer. (A postscript to this story is that later on that year when the winners in fiction were announced that "extraordinary writer" had lost to the peerless Katherine Anne Porter.)

By the middle 1960s I had published three books, two of them novels and one collection of short stories. My third novel and fourth book, *A Dream of Kings,* was published in 1966 by David McKay & Co. The publishers, Kennett Rawson and his wife Eleanor Rawson had been staunch supporters of my work from the time Eleanor held a position as a magazine editor and published several of my stories.

When I submitted the first chapters of *A Dream of Kings,* to David McKay, Eleanor and Kennett Rawson responded with enthusiasm and, heartened, I worked hard to finish.

A Dream of Kings related the story of Leonidas Matsoukas, a stalwart citizen of Greek Town on Chicago's Halsted Street and sole proprietor of the Pindar Master Counseling Clinic. The logo on the door of his shabby office situated above a grocery on Halsted Street read as follows:

PINDAR MASTER COUNSELING SERVICE
Leonidas Matsoukas-President
Doctor of Wisdom and Inspiration
University of Experience
And
College of Life
Palmistry-Astrology-Omen Analysis-
Inspiration to overcome drinking, bed-wetting,
And impotence-Greek poems written for
All occasions-Real Estate Bought and Sold-

Wrestling Instruction (Hellenic Champion
Of Pittsburgh 1947–1948-Vocabulary Tutoring-
Personality Improvement-Talent Agent for
Banzakis Restaurants (Attractive hostesses in
Special demand)
BY APPOINTMENT ONLY

Matsoukas was a fiercely proud man with a zest for life, and a poet's love of language. When the novel begins, he has been married for ten years to his wife, Caliope, who has borne him three children. Two of them, Faith and Hope, are healthy attractive girls. His youngest child, a son, Stavros, has been wracked from birth by an elusive ailment that impedes his growth and weakens his body. The prognosis of the doctors is a gloomy one, ultimately predicting the boy's early death.

Matsoukas stubbornly refuses to accept their somber assessment of his son's fate. Ignoring any medical diagnosis, he believes that if he can transport the child to the vibrant, matchless sun of Greece, his son's illness will be healed.

Caliope believes he is floundering for hope when hope isn't justified. During the years of their marriage, she has also grown weary of Matsoukas's gambling, his numerous get-rich schemes that invariably fail, and his emotional volatility. Among the cruelest of the inflictions he has imposed on her, she also knows him to be unfaithful.

Matsoukas is a loving family man but driven by his volcanic nature and fertile imagination, he is also an incurable romantic, searching for the renewal of love in his attraction to other women.

Matsoukas lives on the periphery of insolvency because of the uncertain income from his counseling service and the erratic flips of fortune he suffers at the gambling tables. Raising enough money to pay the fares for his son and himself to fly to Greece continues to elude him. His desperate efforts to obtain that money and fulfill his dream of Greece saving his son is the core of the story.

While the three books I had published before *Dream* had been well reviewed, the sales for all three were modest. The first hint we had that the reception to *Dream* might be different came in a sheaf of reader's reports collected by David McKay. People spoke of the novel

Chapter 14

as being a "page turner," "vibrant and exciting" and of Matsoukas literally "leaping off the pages." As a consequence of these early plaudits, Eleanor Rawson told me they would be issuing a second printing (which was followed by a third printing) of *Dream* before the official date of publication.

When the book was published, we were rewarded with fine reviews in *Life* and in *Time* and by favorable reviews in other newspapers and magazines.

About a month following publication, like an unexpected blossom in a winter garden, *A Dream of Kings* appeared on the *New York Times* best-seller list. When I first saw it in seventh or eighth place on the list of the top ten, I had to overcome my apprehension that the paper had somehow made an error. I had years before reconciled myself that while writing satisfied my longing to create stories, I would never really earn enough money on which my family could live.

After that auspicious launch onto the *New York Times* list, good news came in daily spurts. The book became an alternate selection for the Doubleday book club. Bantam Books contracted for a paperback edition. Foreign rights were sold in England, France, Germany, and half a dozen other countries. Finally, achieving the crown jewel of any best seller, my agent on the West Coast, Gordon Molson, notified me that he was receiving offers from film companies to turn *Dream* into a film.

I felt as if I were perched on a merry-go-round whirling with ever-increasing speed. After the barren years it was difficult to accept that fortune had turned my way.

Among several film groups bidding for the book was the distinguished production team of John Frankenheimer and Ed Lewis, the director and producer who had optioned my first novel for *Playhouse 90*. There were also offers from several other studios including one from National General Pictures. Their offer, the highest of the lot, had a 48-hour time limit. After a spirited telephone conversation with my agents, we accepted the offer. The $100,000 they paid wasn't that princely a sum by bestseller standards today but in the mid-1960s was an imposing amount. I agreed and the sale was made.

Before the sale of *Dream* to film, my only exposure to Hollywood comprised a trip I made to California in the early 1960s. On that occasion I had received a phone call from a Los Angeles film company called Four-Star Productions. My first response was that it had some link to Four Roses, a quality bourbon I had imbibed on occasion.

The call was from a film director I knew nothing about at the time named Sam Peckinpah and concerned the purchase of the rights to my short story, "Pericles on 31st Street" that first appeared in the *Atlantic*. In addition to their buying the film rights to the story, I was invited to travel to California and to work with Peckinpah, who would be the film's director, on the teleplay. We would adapt the story for a television anthology program, the *Dick Powell Theater*.

A week later I flew to Los Angeles, spent the night in a motel the studio had arranged for me, and the next morning drove to the Paramount Pictures lot and to the offices of Unit Productions.

This new production company comprised three television and film veterans. Bruce Geller, who was responsible for creating the television hits *Mannix* and *Mission: Impossible*. Bernard Kowalski was a director of numerous television films including the pilots for *Richard Diamond Private Detective, The Untouchables*, and the critical hit *N.Y.P.D Blue*. He was also executive producer of *Baretta* and coproducer with Geller of *Mission: Impossible*. The third partner was the film director Sam Peckinpah, known for scores of television productions and, at the time of our meeting, two feature-length films.

Bruce Geller was a tall, handsome man with an engaging laugh. Kowalski was shorter but darkly good-looking with large dark eyes and a wry sense of humor. Sam Peckinpah was slightly built, of medium height, with glowing, expressive eyes. He sported a small mustache and had an animated way of speaking and gesturing when he became excited.

In addition to having directed scores of television episodes, Peckinpah had directed two films. His first, *The Deadly Companions* was a low-budget film shot on location in Arizona. Sam spoke of that film as a learning experience for himself and those who worked with him. The actor, Brian Keith who had appeared in many of the television episodes Sam directed was the male lead and the lovely Maureen O'Hara, an actress I thought stunning, who played the female lead in *The Quiet Man* as well as *How Green Was My Valley*, a film I loved above all others. During the filming of *The Deadly Companions*,

Peckinpah quarreled with the film's producer. As a result of that dissension he vowed never to direct a film again unless he had script control. *The Deadly Companions* may be the least known of Peckinpah's magnificent films.

The second film Peckinpah had directed at the time we met was *Ride the High Country* starring Joel McCrea and Randolph Scott as aging cowboys caught in the turmoil of the changing western frontier.

A week or so after I arrived at the Unit Productions offices, Peckinpah screened *Ride the High Country* for a small group. I emerged from the screening room overwhelmed, thinking the film one of the finest westerns I had ever seen. I did not know then how much the picture's theme of men outliving their own legends and finding in death a redemption of their lives would permeate the films Peckinpah made later in his career.

Peckinpah was justifiably proud of *Ride the High Country*. Entering his office one day, I found him at his desk with a newspaper spread out before him in which a film critic had written glowingly of *Ride the High Country*. Sam passed the paper over to me to read.

"It's a great picture and deserves a fine review, Sam," I said.

"By God, it really does!" Sam laughed.

During those weeks I spent in California I met the man who had first read my story in the *Atlantic* and brought it to the attention of the others. He was the brilliant cinematographer, Lucien Ballard who had seen my story as a viable role for his friend, the actor, Richard Burton. Ballard told us that while visiting his oceanfront home in Zuma Beach, north of Malibu, before a gathering of friends, Burton had read the story aloud. When I recalled Burton's rich, sonorous voice, that reading must have been a treasured experience for those who heard him.

Nothing developed on the story with Burton but Ballard had worked with Peckinpah on *Ride the High Country* and, with the formation of Unit Productions, showed Sam my story. After reading it Sam contacted me.

For the following few weeks I worked daily with Peckinpah, driving each morning from my motel in Hollywood to the house he had rented in Malibu. With the lulling sounds of the ocean drifting through the open windows and the large living room suffused with sunlight, we reviewed the pages of the script I had written the day before.

Looking back on that time we worked together, I understand how much I learned from Sam. In my stories and novels words were the essence of the plot and story and silence had no relevance. Sam taught me the importance of silence in film.

I had written a scene for *Pericles on 31st Street* in which a group of young hoodlums, on the orders of Leonard Barsevick, the corrupt alderman/landlord, as a punishment and a warning, break up the old Greek vendor's hot dog cart.

In dramatizing this scene, I wrote a page of lengthy dialogue in which the old man, frustrated and enraged, vents his anger at the hoodlums, eloquently calling down on their heads the wrath of the old Greek gods.

I was shocked when Peckinpah and I sat down to work over the script to see a bright red marker deleting the entire page of the old Greek's passionate denunciation.

"You've cut all my words, Sam!" I protested. "I worked hard on that scene! That was good dialogue!"

Sam gave me a wry curlicue of a smile.

"It is wonderful dialogue . . . for a novel," he said gently. "But in film you'll see we don't need it."

Peckinpah was absolutely right. In the finished film when old Simonakis comes from the lunchroom to find his wagon in ruins he stands for a moment looking helplessly after the fleeing hoodlums. Peckinpah has the camera pan in on a close-up of the actor's face (the folk-singer Theodore Bikel movingly played Simonakis). His anguish, frustration and rage were clearly visible without the need of a word being spoken.

That may have been the first but wasn't the last lesson on the writing of a film in contrast to the creating of a novel I learned from Sam Peckinpah.

For the following few weeks our daily working routine remained the same. Sam and I would meet at his house in Malibu or in the Unit Production offices on the Paramount lot. He'd make his suggestions for a series of scenes. Afterwards I'd return to my room in the motel and write until evening when Sam would pick me up. We'd have a few drinks (he first introduced me to the beguiling taste of margaritas) and then we'd have dinner in a Hollywood restaurant. Afterwards we'd sit and talk . . . and talk.

In later years when I lectured to university writing classes that often included film students, hearing of the evenings I'd spent with Peckinpah, the students were eager to know what we had discussed night after night, what secrets the great filmmaker might have revealed about his art. The stark truth was that I could not then and still cannot now remember our conversation during those congenial evenings. Perhaps it was the mesmerizing effect of the margaritas or simply the casual rambling. I remember speaking of my early years of writing and Sam speaking of his years of apprenticeship in television and film. We spoke of life, love and death. The evenings brought us close in terms of friendship, but the details of those conversations remain obscured for me to this day.

When the screenplay was completed, Sam began to audition actors for the various roles. Meanwhile, with Bruce Geller and Bernie Kowalski, I began the writing of another project. Bruce had an idea for a series to be called *The Judge* and we set about writing the pilot.

The experience I gained with Sam was further enhanced by Geller's talent. In the weeks we worked together, we established a congenial working relationship much like the one I had developed earlier with Sam.

I'd write during the day in my motel room. In the evening Bruce Geller, sometimes alone, or with Bernie Kowalski would come for a meeting.

As I recall those days I spent writing, I recall that the motel where I lived and worked was also occupied by a group of young aspiring actors and actresses. They spent their days frolicking in and around the pool, undoubtedly waiting for calls from their agents or studios. My balcony on the second floor directly overlooked the pool.

Sometimes as a break from the routine of writing I'd sit on my terrace and watch the young thespians at play. The girls were lovely and flirtatious, the young men handsome and lustful as satyrs.

One of them, short and very muscular, walked with the strut of a bantam rooster. The others called him "Barney." He blatantly pursued all the girls. I watched the sexual games of pursuit and retreat and recall one day hearing one of the girls rebuff Barney by saying, "Oh Barney, you're too short for me."

I can still recall the brash bravado of Barney's response.

"Well, lie down, honey, and watch me grow!"

In the meantime, Peckinpah had finished casting *Pericles on 31st Street*. In addition to Theodore Bikel playing the lead, the major character parts were played by Arthur O'Connell, Strother Martin, Milton Seltzer and Karl Svenson, all talented actors Sam would use again in his later films. In the role of the avaricious and guileful alderman-landlord, Barsevick, Sam cast the talented Carroll O'Connor. This was some time before the actor played his landmark role as Archie Bunker in the television series *All in the Family*.

With the script completed and the cast assembled, the filming of the picture about to begin, early one morning Sam began outlining the routine we'd follow for the daily shooting. He'd provide me a script of the scenes to be shot, and at the end of the day, we'd review the way the shooting of the scenes had gone.

What Sam was offering me then was a remarkable opportunity to work and learn about filmmaking from him. He admired my stories and I believe projected our doing future films together.

But I missed Diana and our sons, missed working on my own stories and didn't really enjoy the skeletal craft of screenplays. That format didn't allow for the versatility of language, a freedom one was allowed in writing a novel.

A little apologetically I said, "Sam, I don't want to stay here for the shooting of the film. I want to go home."

I anticipated Sam might raise an objection but he made no effort to dissuade me, quietly accepting my decision. A few days later I flew back to the Midwest.

In the decades that have passed since then, I think sometimes how the course of my life and the lives of my family might have been altered if I'd stayed in California.

If I had remained for the shooting of *Pericles on 31st Street* or if Sam had raised any strong objection to my leaving, I might have stayed to work with him on that film and on films to follow. My family would have stayed on in California.

If the pilot of *The Judge* had been picked up for a series, my contract with Geller and Kowalski called for me to write four of the season's dozen scripts. I would also function as story editor for the series, with responsibility to assign the remaining scripts to other writers. The money I was to be paid would have been far more than any I had earned before. That largesse would have made it almost impossible to leave California.

By a series of events and decisions that seemed relatively insignificant at the time, the course of a family's life is set. Yet, if we had remained in California, how would my life with Diana have been changed? How would the lives of our sons have been altered? Would the scenario that unfolded for all of us been better or worse?

All that speculation makes little difference now. Even God hasn't the power to undo the past.

Hollywood

PART TWO

The preceding chapter detailed my experiences in Hollywood with the filming of my short story "Pericles on 31st Street." The success of *A Dream of Kings,* which was sold to National General Pictures, brought us back to California in 1966. With the studio paying our substantial rental, Diana, John, Dean and I moved into the spacious ranch house of Bernie Kowalski in the San Fernando Valley. Bernie and his wife Helen were shooting a film in Spain. In a landscape vastly different from the crowded urban neighborhood where we lived in Chicago I began writing the screenplay for *A Dream of Kings.*

While I was working on the script, National General had begun interviewing potential directors. A number of them were eager to have the assignment. The studio settled on Fred Coe, a prestigious director and producer of plays on Broadway and director of the film *A Thousand Clowns.* I found Fred Coe warm, empathetic, and creatively astute. Our collaboration proved fertile. As with the hours I spent with Sam, Fred had a great deal to teach me about film. When I finished the screenplay of *Dream,* the studio executives expressed their delight.

Coe and I both felt that the part of Caliope, the wife of Matsoukas needed a strong, sensual actress who could stand up to the charismatic and powerful Matsoukas. We immediately and enthusiastically agreed on Irene Papas. The studio approved the choice and that wonderful actress was sent the script and she agreed to accept the part. Having admired her greatly in the Greek tragedies she performed, I could not have been more delighted.

Our trouble began with the selection of an actor to play Matsoukas. Soon after the screenplay was finished, I was stunned to learn the studio had offered the part to Dean Martin, an urbane and talented singer-actor but one bearing little resemblance to the stalwart, ebullient Matsoukas. I was relieved when Martin turned the part down.

The studio then offered the role to Omar Sharif. While his dark haired, black-eyed persona was closer to the Matsoukas I had conceived, his polished good looks and reserved manner did not match Matsoukas. Sharif also turned the part down.

With reason-defying logic, the studio then leaped to offer the part to Paul Newman, at the time another box-office star. Coe who had worked with Newman on a previous project went to New York to discuss the film with him. After returning, he conveyed Newman's reaction to playing the role of Matsoukas.

"Look at me," Newman laughed. "A hundred and thirty pounds, dripping wet. If I were to clench my fist and cry out, 'I must take my dying son to Greece,' the audience would burst into laughter! On the other hand if an actor such as Anthony Quinn were to clench his big fist and utter those words, the audience would find him utterly believable."

Newman's mention of Quinn wasn't the first time that epic actor's name had come up to play Matsoukas. Several of the studio executives had suggested Quinn when we first discussed casting for Matsoukas. I had been against him for the role of Matsoukas only because I admired him so much as an actor. I loved his performance in *Viva Zapata,* as the brother of the revolutionary leader, Emiliano Zapata. Above all, I marveled at his incomparable performance in *Zorba the Greek.* In that superb film directed by Michael Cacoyannis, I felt Quinn played *Zorba* so powerfully, that his performance would be compared to and overshadow any other Greek character he played.

However, the more I thought about Quinn playing the part, I began to understand that *Zorba* and *Matsoukas* were starkly different characters. *Zorba* was a peasant, blunt and gruff, a primitive in his philosophy about love and life.

By contrast Matsoukas was an urban artist and a poet. I became convinced that Quinn's superb acting abilities would overcome any comparison to the role he'd played as *Zorba*. I became a champion for the great actor to be offered the role of Matsoukas.

At the time we were considering him for the part of Matsoukas, Anthony Quinn was filming the Morris West novel, *Shoes of the Fisherman,* in Rome. Quinn was playing the Pope. After contacting him through his agent, National General studio executive Irving Levin, Quinn's agent, Fred Coe and I flew to Rome to visit with Quinn at his villa, a magnificent orchard-strewn estate that adjoined the estate of the Pope's summer villa.

When we first met him, Quinn's robust personality seemed to be a vibrant fusion of all the roles he had played in film. He was tall and brawny, with a majestic head on a big, strong frame and with fiery eyes. He was cordial and prone to outbursts of booming laughter. When someone remarked on the quality of the wine we drank from the grapes that had been harvested on his estate, Quinn laughed buoyantly, relating that it cost him twice as much to grow and bottle his wine as he received for its sale. I kept watching him with fascination, seeing in his gestures and range of expressions, a medley of characters he had played in various movies.

A little later while sitting on his terrace overlooking his orchards, Quinn jumped up and waved his hands in greeting to his small blond sons who were approaching with their nanny on a path from the orchards. The gesture was so dramatic and appropriate a portrayal of a father greeting his sons; I looked around expecting to see cameras filming the scene.

We ate an elaborate dinner at Quinn's long dining table joined by his lovely Italian wife. After dinner, continuing to imbibe Quinn's wine, we discussed the script. While expressing his admiration for the novel, at one point Quinn also reproached me by saying, "You give me words I can't speak!"

At the time I remember thinking that was a candid admission of his inadequacies as an actor. It wasn't until later that I understood what Quinn meant. If the dialogue I provided him to speak did not conform to the character he was playing, the words were wrong. If the language were too full of poetic flourish, violating the way the character might naturally speak, the words were wrong. That statement hearkened back to the comment Paul Newman had made when the studio offered him the part of Matsoukas.

Ensconced in my pride about the greatness of my novel and its characters, at the time I thought Quinn wrong. My feeling was that unless he could expand his range as an actor to accommodate my depiction of the character, he had proven himself inadequate for the part.

A few days later I flew home from Rome while Coe stayed on to confer with Quinn on the script. When Coe returned a week later from Rome to Los Angeles, we met to discuss the changes Quinn had demanded. As I was faced with cut after cut, alterations and simplifications in my dialogue that Quinn had insisted upon, I felt my screenplay eviscerated. I responded by becoming angry and obstinate.

I am almost embarrassed to record saying indignantly to Coe some inane babble that long after Quinn's fame had slipped into twilight, my novel would still be read.

Recalling my outburst, I don't remember feeling any uneasiness at my arrogance. I had forgotten that the Greek tragedies abound with cautionary tales of the gods striking down the arrogant, the conceited, and those guilty of the ancient sin of hubris.

No more than a week after that meeting with Coe, who had to report my obstinacy and disapproval about Quinn's suggestions back to the studio, we were driving from Beverly Hills back to our home in the Valley. Our son John, who had gotten into the habit of reading *The Hollywood Reporter,* spoke from the back seat.

"Hey Pa, they just kicked you off *A Dream of Kings!*"

That statement from my son delivered bluntly from the back seat while I was driving seventy miles an hour along a Los Angeles freeway, struck me with the impact of an oncoming car.

Citing dismissal provisions in our contract, the studio had indeed fired me. That comprised my lesson in the protocol of Hollywood whereby in any conflict between writer and star, the outcome was inevitable. When the studio signed Quinn for the part of Matsoukas, they fired me as writer.

Caught between the demands of the studio and his loyalty to me as the novel writer and a friend, Fred Coe opted not to direct the film.

He resigned from the project. I lamented that decision because his view of story and characters was much like mine. A new director, Daniel Mann, was chosen.

In retrospect, after a passage of so many years, I realized that I was wrong. Anthony Quinn knew his strengths and his limitations as an actor and, in support of his position, simply exercised his power. Instead of obstinately defying him, I should have initially made an effort to understand his objections and, to whatever degree I could, accommodate to his wishes. I would have remained involved with the filming, and I would have been able to exercise whatever influence I could on the way the character was portrayed.

Later on, Anthony Quinn and I forged our peace. During the filming of *A Dream of Kings,* the company on location filmed for about a week on Halsted Street in Chicago. I visited the set then with the film's producer, Jules Schermer, and met the lovely Inger Stevens who played the Widow Anthoula. I also visited with Quinn again. He was cordial and complimentary and I wished him the best of luck with the role.

The first few times I viewed the finished film of *A Dream of Kings,* I was disheartened, anguishing about the facets of character, language and story that had been lost in the conversion from the novel into film. I also admit that in the years that have passed since then, each successive viewing chipped away at that disapproval.

If I had remained involved with the project, we might have made a film closer to the vision of the novel. Still, the talents of Anthony Quinn and Irene Papas created a passionate and memorable relationship on screen. Their scenes seethed with power and smoldered with sensuality. In addition, the scenes of Quinn speaking of the healing sun of Greece while holding his frail, dying son in his arms were poignant and memorable.

I met Anthony Quinn again in the 1980s, after I'd written and published *Ghost of the Sun,* a novel-sequel to *A Dream of Kings* using the same characters I had written about in *Dream.* Quinn had read the book and phoned me to convey his enthusiasm. I told him I'd send along some of the reviews. His response was emphatic.

"I don't need to see any reviews! You've written a goddam beautiful book! Let's make the film!"

In the year that followed we endeavored in vain to get a screenplay commissioned and make a film of *Ghost of the Sun*. We had a problem with Warner Brothers Studio that had bought the rights to the original novel. They raised one objection after another to thwart our efforts. Quinn had trouble with that studio in the past and felt they were obstructing our efforts out of spite.

In this span of time Quinn came to Chicago to do a play. While he was in the city, we arranged a meeting with him along with my son John. John and I had worked together on a couple of my shorter pieces produced for television, and we planned to work together on *Ghost*.

We spent the afternoon discussing the project with Quinn. About halfway through we went downstairs to the hotel grill for lunch. The lunch hour had passed and fewer than half a dozen patrons still lingered.

First, a young woman came over, telling Quinn how much she admired his work and would he please grant her his autograph. Quinn signed a piece of paper for her.

A few moments later a man came over to tell Quinn how much his son admired Quinn's work. Would Tony please sign an autograph for his son? Quinn obliged.

After another five to ten minutes, two men sitting at the bar approached our booth. One of them sported a glistening gold watch chain dangling from the pocket of his vest.

"Tony," the man said with a wide-toothed smile. "My buddy here and I got a bet. You can settle it for us."

Quinn waited in silence and the man hurtled on.

"Didn't you fuck Irene Papas in *The Guns of Navarone*?"

I sat there in shock and heard Quinn say quietly.

"No . . ."

The man frowned and the two men walked away. A few moments later a waiter came over to say the gentlemen at the bar wished to buy the three of us a drink. What was our pleasure?

Quinn said, "no." I quickly followed with "no" and my son said "no."

As we were leaving the hotel that afternoon, we said goodbye to Quinn in the lobby.

"Listen to your son," Quinn admonished me. "He understands what I'm looking for in the character of Matsoukas better than you do."

The project dragged on and, finally, floundered. One day I received a letter from Quinn's lawyer telling me the actor was no longer interested in developing the project.

Having missed the opportunity to work with Quinn on *Dream* one of the deep regrets of my life was losing the opportunity to work with that marvelous actor on *Ghost of the Sun.*

The most gratifying part of the nearly two years we spent in Hollywood were the friendships we developed. Among these friends were Dorothy and Peter Bart. At the time Bart was an executive associate of Robert Evans who led Paramount Studios. The two men had been instrumental in developing the project that became the magnificent *Godfather* trilogy directed by Francis Ford Coppola.

Through the hospitality and friendship of Dorothy and Peter, Diana and I attended private studio screenings of newly completed films. We sat in small projection rooms with, at different times, Jack Lemmon, Water Matthau, Kirk Douglas, James Coburn, Sally Field, Debbie Reynolds, and other legendary film actors and actresses. The custom in such screening rooms mandated that no one was introduced or spoken to unless spoken to first so we never actually met any of these stars. Although I have never been a collector of autographs, to have asked for one at those screenings would have been a gross violation of the proprieties. I would look at these legendary figures admiringly, recalling the many memorable film characters they had played that I had enjoyed.

We did meet certain stars, writers and directors when Dorothy and Peter Bart invited us to one of their splendid dinners. I find it hard now to remember just which guests were present except for a memorable evening when we met the lovely Ali McGraw.

I also recall one guest I wished I could have met that we missed. Dorothy Bart had asked us to join them for a dinner they were planning for Mario Puzo, the author of *The Godfather.* I was eagerly looking forward to meeting the celebrated author and had several writing (as well as gambling) questions I wished to ask him. When we arrived, Dorothy told us that, at the last minute, Puzo had decided to make a fast trip to Las Vegas.

There was one memorable meeting with Paul Newman. Remembering the concerns he had expressed to Fred Coe about playing Matsoukas, some months after *A Dream of Kings* had been completed, I heard Paul Newman was shooting a film at one of the Hollywood studios. I phoned the studio and left my name. A while later a secretary phoned back with an invitation for me to meet Newman on the set.

He was as handsome a man in person as he appeared in films with his legendary large blue eyes. He was warm and gracious and kept pressing me for details of my experience with the writing and filming of *A Dream of Kings*. From time to time he lubricated our conversation with another can of cold beer from a large cooler in the corner of his dressing room.

Each time they called him to shoot another scene, I rose to leave. Each time he urged me to stay and, after shooting his scene, he returned to the dressing room and we resumed our conversation and continued drinking more beer.

Only on my drive from the studio back to our valley home did the awesome reality strike me that I had been sitting, conversing and drinking cans of beer with Cool Hand Luke!

There were also dinners and the nurturing of a deep friendship with David Westheimer who wrote *Von Ryan's Express,* a wonderful novel that had been made into a dramatic film starring Frank Sinatra. I had met David a few years earlier at one of the midwestern writers' conferences where we both taught. When we settled in California, we resumed our friendship. Through David and Dody we also met the talented husband and wife writing team of Kay and Jess Carneal. The six of us lubriciously celebrated numerous dinners together.

The dearest friendship I formed during our stay in Hollywood was with the wonderful character actor of Hellenic heritage, Nick Dennis. I met him for the first time in one of the offices at Paramount studios. He was short in height, with a great head, his features seemingly carved in rock, and with the brawny arms and shoulders of a weightlifter. The first impression one had of Nick was his ebullience. He did not speak words but hurled them out of his broad chest.

Nick had an extensive film and drama background, acting in dozens of roles on stage and in film. He had played one of the principal gladiators with Kirk Douglas in *Spartacus*, and had played in *A Street-car Named Desire*, on Broadway. He had costarred with the actor, Jack Palance in *The Big Knife*.

I invited Nick to dinner at our house the following Friday. When he entered our house that night and confronted our sons, John and Dean, he mimicked a Chicago gangster, snarling, and "A couple of toughs from Chicago! Well, you guys take this!" Nick bent his arms in imitation of a man holding a tommy gun, "Bbbbbrrrrrrroooom-bang!" Our sons loved him at once.

Diana had cooked an all-Greek meal that included dolmades and pastitsio that evening, the first Greek food Nick told us he had eaten in quite a while. He was effusive in his praise, going so far as to pledge to kill anyone Diana wished eliminated. When I cautioned Nick that her death list might include me, he stared at me in shock and then commented. "Ahhh, you writers . . . always plotting!" We were all charmed by Nick and Diana invited him to return for dinner again the following Friday.

Nick did return and, after first phoning to ask Diana's permission, brought with him Chris Marks, an older distinguished-looking character actor with a bushy head of white hair.

"Chris Marks is a great guy!" Nick had told Diana. "He's been around forever. You'll love him and he'll love you!

We did indeed come to admire and love Chris Marks who played a small character part in *A Dream of Kings*.

Every Friday night for months following that first dinner, a growing number of actors, musicians, and other artists assembled around our table. Looking back on that contingent of visitors, I marvel how Diana could have managed to prepare the meals for so many on her own. Everyone who ate at her table became her enthusiastic fan and admirer.

In addition to Nick and Chris Marks, our visitors included Jim Harakas, a marvelous guitarist, who in the service of U.S. Intelligence had parachuted behind enemy lines in France in World War II. What was unique about his jump is that he made it carrying his guitar. Others who joined the weekly dinners were Peter Mamakos, Ben Sawyer, Larry Phillips, and a number of other actors whose names I can no longer remember. None were stars but all were seasoned professionals who had appeared in many films. Their stories about their struggles to make it in their chosen profession were poignant and unforgettable. Yet none of them would have thought of giving up.

Chris Marks, the old veteran thespian, speaking of his ongoing struggle to survive as an actor, told me pensively one night, "The last happy year of my life was 1929 when I sang in *The Student Prince* for the Schuberts."

"Why not try another profession, Chris?" I rashly suggested. "You are bright and personable. I'm sure you'd do well in any number of occupations."

Chris looked at me reproachfully, drew himself to his full imposing height, and said quietly, "I'm an actor. That is my profession."

I felt properly rebuked.

Included among those who came and ate at our table was a young actor who had written a 300-page screenplay, three times the length of an average feature film, titled *Who's Calling?*

The question referred to the scores of times he had phoned studios, casting directors, and agents in an effort to find work. The identical response from a phone operator or secretary were those two blunt words, "Who's calling?" When he spoke his name, that ended the phone call.

He had vented all his years of resentments and humiliations into that bulky, impossible to ever make screenplay that he carried around with him as if it were a bomb he hoped to detonate.

Those Friday dinners were memorable events for Diana and for me. The evening would begin with an array of visitors announcing their arrival by strolling up our driveway, often led by Jim Harakas playing his guitar and singing some bawdy lyrics. He was joined by other musicians including a fine tenor and by a saxophonist. I also remember a juggler and a magician.

One evening, Nick Dennis and Jim Harakas robustly performed the Karaghoizi, the Greek shadow theater using hand-manipulated puppets behind a white screen. They skillfully alternated the voices of the principal characters in a dramatic performance.

As Diana and I were going to bed that evening I told her:

"Watching Nick and Jim do that play tonight is going to give me a story."

I cannot recall how long after that night I wrote the story of a puppet master whose profession was no longer viable, leaving him in despair because he was unable to practice his art any longer. That story, "Dark Eye," was published in *Playboy*.

However large the group, Diana was somehow able to miraculously prepare and serve the needed quantities of food so no one ever left hungry.

One memorable night, Nick Dennis brought the actor Jack Palance to dinner. The tall, rugged Palance was cordial and outgoing, telling Diana over and over how much he enjoyed her cooking. Before leaving that night he made a final foray into the kitchen for a last taste of Diana's *dolmades*, the savory Greek dish of rice and meat enveloped in grape leaves.

Near the end of our second year in Hollywood, after we'd made the decision and were packing to leave California, Nick Dennis helped me transport several boxes to the UPS station for shipment back to Chicago. When we'd finished checking them in, and it was time to separate, we embraced, both of us with tears in our eyes.

AFTER THAT PARTING, although we corresponded a few times, I never saw Nick Dennis again. Meanwhile, I will always associate him with the more pleasant aspects of our California sojourn and remember him as being one of the most spontaneous, warm and loving human beings I have ever known.

After writing the screenplay for *A Dream of Kings,* I moved to Paramount to write a treatment and screenplay for a film based on the life of the legendary gambler, Nicholas Andreas Dandolas, known as "Nick the Greek."

The dramatic rights to the gambler's life had been acquired by Eddie Silverman, a Chicago theater owner. He had formed an affiliation with a producer named Bernard Schwartz, who had produced *The Breakfast Club* and *St. Elmo's Fire*.

I moved into the writers' building on the Paramount lot and began working on a treatment. The offices around me were occupied by writers working on other projects. I came to know a number of them but aside from Christopher Knopf, I cannot remember the names of all those toilers in the vineyards of Hollywood.

During my second month of writing on *Nick the Greek*, a young actress named Ina Balin came into my office to introduce herself. She visited on a cloudy California afternoon. When she entered my office, she created a vision of stunning beauty dressed in a fetching white dress so ornately trimmed it might have made a bride's garment. Her face framed by her radiant black hair was one of the loveliest I had ever seen.

She was making the rounds visiting various writers checking to see whether their projects might require her as an actress. After she had departed, the clouds and shadows returned to their dominance, making my surroundings once more dismal and bleak.

As I returned to my writing, I tried extraordinarily hard to create a female character that might be played by the lovely Ina Balin. To my everlasting regret, that effort failed.

Meanwhile, as our family sought to adjust to living in Hollywood, slowly, insidiously, the culture of the community began making an impact.

As I lunched with other writers and producers, all of them seemed to be more affluent and successful than I was. They spoke of purchasing new cars, Mercedes and BMWs. They talked of weekends on Catalina Island and of the fine cuisine of elegant new restaurants they frequented. Without being conscious of what was happening I seemed to be absorbing the status symbols that existed in the Hollywood culture.

Driving with Diana and our sons to a restaurant with valet parking, I was conscious how our five-year old Chevrolet stood out glaringly between a Mercedes in front of us and a BMW behind us. As I handed the valet my keys I felt him scrutinizing my auto and thinking, "This guy is a loser."

The parking area that served our writers' building on the Paramount lot was about a block away. Walking with another writer to my car to drive to a restaurant outside the lot, he commented how far away from the building my parking spot was located.

"This isn't far," I replied. "Less than a block and we have sunshine to walk in every day."

He mentioned the names of a pair of other writers, both of whom, he told me, were parked closer to our building.

"Your parking determines your status," the writer told me gravely. "Those writers are not as good as you, nor are they working on a project as important as yours, but both their cars are parked closer. People see that and evaluate you accordingly."

"That shit doesn't count with me," I scoffed. "Who cares about stuff like that?"

But that night, I found myself brooding about the two lesser-talented writers with better parking slots. I voiced my complaint to Diana who sensibly brushed it aside as nonsense.

The night nourished my grievance and the following day I carried my complaint into the office of my producer, Bernie Schwartz. He looked at me with the resigned expression of a man forced to suffer the vagaries of fools and then, if I remember correctly, mollified me by moving me a space or two closer to the building.

Another writers' building experience came while I was standing in the bathroom at a urinal beside a man who was singing loudly and buoyantly as he voided.

"You must be feeling pretty good," I said.

"Damn good!" he said jubilantly. "First, I imagine myself pissing on my agent! Then I'm pissing on my girlfriend who left me for another guy. Then one final burst on the lunchroom owner who cut off my credit!"

One more fleeting image from those days in the writer's compound is of two men walking swiftly along the hallway of the building. One of them I knew as a burly-bodied producer of small budget films and the other a smaller, nervous man who was an actor's agent. As they passed, the agent trying frantically to keep up with the producer's longer strides, I caught a snatch of their exchange.

"What I need is a young Paul Newman!" the producer barked.

"I got him, Lionel!" the agent cried. "I swear to God I got him!"

When I completed a 100-page story on Nick the Greek, it appeared we would move forward to write a screenplay and make a film. Robert Evans, the head of Paramount, and his administrative assistant, Peter Bart, were enthusiastic about the story. In the end, disappointing to myself as well as to Eddie Silverman and Bernie Schwartz, Paramount decided against further development.

In the final negotiations, I was granted literary rights to the story I had written. Based on my treatment, I went on to write a novel that was published in 1976 by Doubleday under the title, *Nick the Greek*.

The story I'd written on Nick the Greek was based on a real person, Nicholas Andreas Dandolos, who had been born in Crete, Greece in 1883 and died in Los Angeles on Christmas Day, 1966. His life, ornamented by the years he gambled and his exploits mythologized in the years following his death is probably a fusion of truth and legend.

In his lifetime as a high-stakes gambler Nick was reputed to have played in games that involved winning and losing millions of dollars. These games were sometimes marathons that lasted weeks and even months against notorious gamblers such as Arnold Rothstein and Johnny Moss. Nor did Nick always win. He was known for the magnitude of his losses as well as the size of his winnings.

In Las Vegas, every dealer, and pit boss I spoke to had a Nick the Greek story. One called him 'generous' and another referred to him as 'miserly.' One said he had a 'genial nature' and another referred to him as having a 'volatile temper.'

In the final years of his life, having won and lost fortunes, Nick ended up impoverished, his health precarious and his eyesight failing.

But Nick was an institution in Las Vegas and the casino owners were reluctant to allow him to fade away. They subsidized him, providing him room and board and pocket money to keep him playing at their tables. When tourists to Las Vegas descended from plane or train and were asked what they wished to see first of all, their response was "Boulder Dam and Nick the Greek gambling." The casino that had Nick playing at one of their roulette or poker tables drew many of these tourists.

Despite the huge sums of money that had passed through his hands, Nick died poor and alone in a shabby Los Angeles hotel on Christmas Day, 1966. The casino owners in one final, zealous effort to exploit his reputation transported him from Los Angeles to Las Vegas in a golden hearse. For the dead gambler, they orchestrated a grand funeral befitting a king. The governor and lt. governor of Nevada were there and dealers and pit bosses working in the casinos were given time off to attend the rites. Ed Sullivan, host of *Talk of the Town*, came from New York and a number of movie stars from Hollywood were also present. Frank Sinatra came to the funeral and was reported to have wept for the deceased gambler.

Hank Greenspun, publisher of the *Las Vegas Sun* announced Nick's death with a headline in the paper and, at the funeral, eulogized Nick, saying, "Nick loved Las Vegas and Las Vegas loved Nick."

Jim Harakas, who became a good friend of our family and who joined the Friday night dinners in our California house, was also the nephew of Nick the Greek. Before Nick's death, Jim had spent considerable time with the gambler in Las Vegas.

While I worked on the story of Nick the Greek, Jim Harakas and I made several trips together to Las Vegas so he could introduce me to some of the gamblers and pit bosses who remembered Nick.

On one of those early trips to Las Vegas, Jim took me to the Woodlawn Cemetery where Nick was interred. We found Nick's grave to be a barren patch of ground marked only with a postcard-sized metal nameplate reading simply *Nick the Greek*. On the day we visited the cemetery, the grave held a small sprig of fresh flowers.

In the cemetery office we were told that the metal nameplate had been placed on Nick's grave because earlier plastic ones were being stolen by souvenir hunters. We asked who might have put the fresh flowers on the grave and the office manager summoned a groundskeeper. The man, who was of Greek descent, confessed he had never known Nick the Greek but heard he was a famous Greek gambler. As a sign of respect, from time to time, when a funeral cortege arrived at the cemetery, the groundskeeper took a few fresh flowers from that grave to place on Nick's grave. He told his story nervously as if fearing he would be punished for his transgression. The cemetery manager assured him he wouldn't be punished.

The disheartening postscript to this story is that not one of the millionaire casino owners who had exploited and benefited by Nick's presence and his reputation considered spending a few hundred dollars to place a modest tombstone on the gambler's grave.

I made a vow that I fulfilled after my novel *Nick the Greek* was published. I had a plaque made and placed on Nick's grave that reads "Nicholas Andreas Dandolos, Nick the Greek, 1883–1966." The marker held the images of two dice, the numbers six and five adding to eleven, and, finally, the words, "Gambler and Sage."

If there is any moral to Nick the Greek's story, it is that God help you if Las Vegas loves you.

If Paramount had decided to proceed with making a film of *Nick the Greek,* that assignment would have kept our family in California. Another project that would also have mandated our remaining was the TV pilot I developed with Bruce Geller, on a story called *The Judge.* Geller and I completed a script that Bernie Kowalski directed, starring the fine actor Richard Basehart playing the title role. The pilot appeared on the *Dick Powell Anthology Theater.*

Although the script won a Writer's Guild Drama Award, the pilot wasn't bought by any of the networks. If the story had been sold, my services as writer and story editor would have been so financially lucrative it would have been senseless to turn it down.

If we had remained in California, I would have continued writing screenplays, unquestionably made a good deal more money, and, as a result, our family would have endured less economic hardship than we experienced after we returned to Chicago.

But if we had stayed in that volatile environment, the Hollywood culture rife with temptations, my wife and I might not have remained together. Our sons would have been raised in radically altered circumstances, and chosen other careers. They would have met and married different girls than our beloved daughter-in-laws. And, most somber of all scenarios, I might never have written another novel or short story.

Epilogue

My first visit to Greece took place in 1968 when I traveled there with Diana and two of our sons. We made additional trips during the 1970s and 1980s to visit our beloved relatives on the island of Crete. On a half dozen other trips, I traveled alone to Greece.

The last trip Diana and I made to Greece together was in 2004. By chance we shared a cataclysmic event taking place at that time when the Greek soccer team, a 100 to 1 entry in the Eurocup, beat France in the semifinals and Portugal in the finals to win the European championship. We witnessed a tumultuous jubilation the Greeks hadn't experienced since they defeated the Persian army at Marathon.

On one of the early trips I made alone to Greece, Christos Karamichos, a friend who owned a Flokati rug shop in Constitution Square in Athens, took me to a taberna named Pale Diamond in the Plaka. That neighborhood in the heart of Athens drew tourists to its tabernas, restaurants, jewelry stores, and souvenir arcades.

The entrance to the Pale Diamond taberna was off Adrianou Street, through an alley and down a flight of basement stairs. A dingy wooden sign hanging above the door had the lettering effaced by weather and time, so only a "P" and "D" were legible.

The interior of the taberna was a cavernous room, shabby and barren except for a dozen wooden tables. A curtain hung along one wall and an old upright piano occupied a corner. A straight-backed chair stood in forlorn solitude in the center of the room. The patrons seated at the tables appeared to be native Greeks.

"Why aren't there any tourists here?" I asked.

"The guides lure foreigners to the fancy emporiums of the Plaka," Christos sneered. "Places where the tables have linen cloths, and the waiters wear clean aprons. Those scoundrels charge a hundred drachmas for a glass of ouzo. This taberna is for Greeks only."

Christos and I sipped glasses of ouzo, but I avoided a platter of limp appetizers that I could not distinguish as either meat or fish.

Men and women at the surrounding tables drank and spoke in hushed tones, a variation from the animated, contentious voices of Greeks when they ate and drank.

"Why are we here, Christos?" I voiced my dismay. "The atmosphere is funereal. Does a relative of yours own this place?"

"Everyone is waiting," Christos said.

"For what?"

"For Sotiris Paleomantis," Christos spoke the name with reverence. "He is the last of the great troubadours."

Moments later, a man carrying a guitar emerged from behind the curtains. He was an old man who walked with a slow, weary tread. He wore a gray suit so worn that the trouser knees and coat sleeves glistened. His shirt had an open collar.

The closer he came, the more ancient he appeared, his ridged face resembling a ravaged bas-relief from a Greek temple. His disheveled white hair was streaked with a few darker, fading strands.

The old man seated himself on the chair, placed the guitar on his knees as carefully as if it were a child, and began to play. As the first resonant tones of the guitar vibrated through the room, he began to sing. His voice was hoarse and uneven and yet imbued with a raw power. He sang what he called the "Song of my Life."

I had difficulty accepting that hyperbole as within the capability of a voice and a guitar. But as the old man played and sang, his words and music joined to evoke images. I shared his childhood exuberance as he splashed in the waves of the sea, followed him through his youth and the lovely girls he courted. His words grew somber as he sang of grief and suffering in war, lost friendships, and the fading of dreams.

Then, as if the guitar and his voice had reached their zenith and could no longer encompass what he still wished to convey, the old man rose to his feet and placed his guitar across the chair. A young waiter seated himself at the piano and his fingers touched the keys. As the music of the piano resounded through the room, Paleomantis began to dance.

His head bent, the troubadour gazed at the floor, extended his arms, flexed his fingers. He began slowly, his figure dipping and turning, his movements stiff and yet still retaining a vestige of the grace with which he must have danced as a youth.

As he bent toward the floor, the fingers of his hand brushed the heel of his shoe. His figure lurched upright, he raised his arm, and his fingers touched his forehead. Down and up, back and forth, his body twisting in an effort obstructed by the stiffness of his limbs. His dance conveyed a spirit defiant and unyielding before the onslaught of age.

When the old troubadour finished his dance, for several moments the audience hung in an awed, breathless silence. Then they erupted into vociferous applause, men emitting strident whistles and cheers while some of the women threw flowers. I joined others who had leaped to their feet, clapping so hard my palms ached.

Nearly fifty years have passed since that night in the Plaka, when through music, song, and dance, the last of the great troubadours conveyed his life in a span of less than an hour. I have now spent a year and written seventy thousand words in an effort to do the same.

I no longer work upstairs in the spacious, light-suffused studio where I have written my books for so many years. In the small downstairs room where I now write to be near my frail wife, the heater glowing at my feet, the sky outside my windows is dark with the imminence of snow.

I began this book last winter and wrote through the following spring, summer and autumn. Now, in the cold and snow of a second winter that is faltering toward spring, I continue foraging for words to filter the multitude of memories. A revered ancestor, the philosopher Plato, writes of all learning as remembering.

Yet, in rereading these pages I have spent these last twelve months writing, I am disheartened at how much is absent. So many adventures and misadventures unrecorded. The passage of myriad birthdays and the annual holidays of Easter, Thanksgiving and Christmas celebrated with our large and extended family. Each dear family member, each nephew and niece, great-nephew and great-niece, deserves a page.

Epilogue

While my own life was unfolding, there were momentous events affecting the world. The Great Depression of the 1930s, World War II engulfing Europe and Pearl Harbor bringing America into the conflict. The detonation of the first atomic bombs at Hiroshima and Nagasaki ending the war with Japan. The launching of satellites into space. The Korean War and the Vietnam War. The Civil Rights struggle, the assassinations of Martin Luther King, Jr., President John Kennedy and Robert Kennedy. September 11, 2001 and the invasions of Iraq and Afghanistan. The election of the first African American president. Those were the events all mankind experienced, while I work on a miniature canvas covering only my life.

I am dismayed at how much of my life is still missing. There is nothing in these pages about the friendships that have enriched my life, many of them with men and women I have been graced to know since our days together in grade school. Nothing as well about so many dear ones who have died.

Except for my brother Dan there is little about my other siblings, their lives and their deaths. Their moving stories may have to wait for other books, perhaps books to be written by their own offspring.

I have written little about my sons who are now grown men and of the lovely women they married. No more than a few scant words about my beloved grandchildren. And, finally, nothing about the myriad travels Diana and I have made across the earth's continents and oceans.

I suppose I have resisted writing too extensively about our sons for fear of damning them with too much praise. The truth is that all three are now mature men ranging in age from 55 to 65. They have been loving, devoted and loyal offspring. They have the exemplary mother they deserve, but I sometimes feel they might have had a better father.

I have written about the economic hardship we endured in the early years, and my suicidal depression when I planned to end my life, leaving my wife a widow and my sons fatherless. I haven't written about our son John's painful illness and depression while a student at Kalamazoo College. Neither Diana or I had any experience with depression then, and our family passed an agonizing few years until our son recovered.

However erratic my employment record while I was trying to write, and the economic insecurity that impacted our lives, our sons were not unhappy. There was always food on our table. The boys had school, (despite their occasional grousing) after-school activities and their own nurturing friendships. All three were actively involved in tennis, baseball and basketball. From their adolescence, all three sons showed interest and talent in theater and in writing.

What sustained our family was Diana being an energetic and devoted mother with little interest in social activities such as those volunteer efforts that absorbed my mother's life. Blunting my own vagaries, my wife's good sense and steadfast nature were the glue that held our home together.

Mark, the eldest, was the first of our sons to leave home, taking flight from the Midwest to settle in northern California. Mark loved and lived for a decade with a talented, vivacious girl named Julie Hebert. Julie, whom I will regard as my daughter for as long as I live, gave birth to the first of our grandchildren, the jewel, Alexis, now a grown woman and recently married.

John moved from Indiana to live and work in Chicago. Then our youngest son Dean left, following his older brother Mark to California. In the next few years John married Carolyn "Linnie" Harnach and they had a son, Lucas. In that same year Dean married Anna Marie Joyner and they had a son, Nicholas and a daughter Adriana.

Each of our sons and their families are living their private joys and sorrows since I am not privy to the intimate aspects of their relationships. As for our relationship with them, writing for Diana and for myself, I cannot list a single grievance either of us have any reason to level against our sons.

Our relationship is marked by wry humor and gentle teasing, sometimes in short, snappy letters, at other times in longer philosophical musings. We have often resorted to the exchange of humorous verse. Utilizing the unsettling swiftness of e-mail, we might transmit a half-dozen messages and poems back and forth in the course of a day.

I include here a few verses I wrote for my sons on Father's Day in June of 2008. These have no literary merit, but are merely an example of sentiments freely exchanged.

WRITTEN FOR OUR BELOVED SONS ON FATHER'S DAY

With apologies to Browning and Longfellow
This father and mother,
Have three peerless sons
Good siblings, good fathers,
No need to make puns

The years we have shared
I will not be coy
Have provided us pride,
And affection and joy.

Through childhood into manhood
We watched each son grow
Felt their love and devotion
Fill our hearts with a glow.

Now we're aging together
Our sons kind, mature men
Each one with great charm
And a flair with the pen.

Long after we're gone,
May good memories linger on,
Of their sweet, loving mother,
And their two-penny Don.

To which our son Mark responded:

Thanks pop!
I love it when you drop
a line or two
gazing and reminiscing
with a rhyme or few,
over and upon..
the cool papa licks
of the two-penny Don.

Our family's first trip to Greece and to my father and mother's island birthplace of Crete took place in August of 1968, when with Diana, John, and Dean, we shared a charter flight I later described in an article as "winged steerage." But the disappointment of the flight with its scarcity of food, shortage of water, and the clogging of its toilets were forgotten as the plane began its descent over Athens. Along with other passengers peering out the plane windows, we caught our first sight of the illuminated Parthenon in a raven-black sky. The temple appeared an apparition of beauty and flame floating in the firmament, a stunning image that embodied all the glory of the Greek past.

After sleeping that first night on Greek soil, the following morning we walked around Athens. The sidewalk cafes at that time, decades before today's economic chaos, flourished with laughter and jubilant voices. At little tables in Syntagma Square, men and women sipped from tumblers of ouzo and tiny cups of Greek coffee, their hands accenting their voices, laughing, scoffing and pontificating.

After several days in Athens, we traveled by tour bus along the national highway. Later in the afternoon we stopped at Delphi, the temple built on the slopes of Mt Parnassus, overlooking the Gulf of Corinth. In the distance, visible on the slopes of the mountains, was a great forest of cypress and olive trees.

Delphi was once the destination for Greeks seeking counsel on love and war from the revered and feared oracles who dwelt there. According to mythology, Delphi was formed when Zeus released twin eagles at opposite ends of the world and they met at the site. The ancients regarded Delphi as the center of the world.

The innkeeper in the small pension where we stayed told us that the spirit of those oracles still lingered in the cliffs and canyons around us.

"Open your windows," he said gravely, "and you will hear their voices in the wind."

I took his somber projection as fodder for tourists, but as twilight misted the mountainside and an eerie wind rattled the shutters on the windows, I heard those ghostly voices.

In the following days we toured the historical sites we had studied in Greek parochial school. The battleground of Marathon with its blood-soaked earth marking a great conflict in 490 B.C. when an army of 9000 Greeks and 1000 Plataeans defeated a 25,000 strong Persian army. After the battle, a runner was dispatched to inform the citizens of Athens of the great victory. The courier's final words to the Athenian assembly before he fell dead of exhaustion were *"Enikesame!"* "We won!"

In imitation of the epic race that warrior made to carry the triumphant news, our sons ran back and forth across the fields.

We visited the site of another great battle in the mountains at Thermopylae where King Leonidas and his 300 Spartans held the pass against the invading Persians until the last warrior had perished. We stood on the heights overlooking the sea battle at Salamis, the surging waves shrouding the wrecks of sunken galleys when Greece defeated the Persian fleet.

We visited Mycenae, the kingdom mighty Agamemnon ruled, on a day when a dark, burdened sky shrouded the peaks of the Lion Gate. I thought perhaps such an overcast sky greeted the king the day he returned from Troy to be murdered by his wife Clytemnestra, and her lover Aegisthus.

Traveling still deeper into the heart of the Peloponnesus, we stood among the ruins of temples in the warrior enclaves of Sparta. Further south and east, we drove alongside the majestic coastal mountain of Monemvasia.

We returned to Athens to pursue our plans to spend Easter in Crete. This would be our first visit to the island birthplace of my father and mother and to meet relatives we knew only from old faded photographs and scrawled letters our parents had shared with us when we were children.

On the morning of Holy Friday, we flew from Athens to Chanea, Crete, the city at the western tip of the island. Having been notified of our impending visit, twoscore relatives gathered to meet us. They came to the airport in cars, by taxi, perched on donkeys, riding wagons and motorbikes. Diana and I and our sons were embraced by emotional men and women who held other family-related names beside Petrakis . . . Christoulakis, Tzangarakis, Mamalakis, Kotsifakis. The cheeks of our sons turned scarlet from the flurry of vigorous, affectionate pinching.

From Chanea, we were driven to my father's village, Argyroupolis, a settlement perched high in the island's majestic White Mountains. There we were greeted by still another swarm of relatives, embraced and hugged, everyone including Diana and me in tears.

"I was boyhood friend to your father!" one man told us.

"I attended your parents' wedding!" a woman said.

"Father Petrakis baptized me!"

"What a voice your father had! On Sunday mornings, people would travel miles from other villages to hear him!"

Antonia Couides, our first cousin, robust and affectionate lady, smothered us in her sturdy arms. Her smiling and effusive husband Yiannis seated us in his coffeehouse and brought us coffee and platters of assorted *mezedes*. My father's brother, my Uncle Manolis, also a priest, his features beneath his white hair and white beard were starkly similar to those of my father. The sturdy priest hugged me so tightly I felt smothered in the scents of incense and candles rising from his black cassock.

I slept that night in the bed my father was born in, heard the rain on the roof he must have listened to as a boy, rose at dawn to mountain air scented with the moist aroma of dew-splashed flowers.

On the Saturday night of the Anastasis, the small church was crowded with village families. The chanting of the liturgy, the glowing of the candles, the scents of candles and incense hurled me back to the church of my childhood.

At midnight, the church interior was snapped into darkness. In that pitch-black interior, a solitary candle was lit, and from that single candle a hundred more fluttered into flame.

As the service ended several hours after midnight, we emerged from the church in the midst of villagers who carried candles, their hands shielding the tiny flickering flames from the wind. The fragrant Cretan night was garlanded by a procession of men, women and children, their passage marked by scores of tiny candle flames weaving through the darkness.

We arrived at my uncle's house and sat down to Easter dinner. With his eyes glowing mischievously, Fr. Manolis offered me the Easter delicacy, the head of the baked lamb.

"Fage, paidi mou, fage!" he cried. "Eat, my boy, eat!"

Epilogue

When my timid gorge refused, he pounced upon the hapless head and devoured it, his tongue scooping the eyes from the skull, and then finishing by exultantly licking the tips of his fingers.

The day after Easter, we drove from Argyroupolis down the mountain into the old city of Rethymnon. Looming in the sky above the city were the minarets of its numerous mosques that evoked the centuries when Greece endured Ottoman rule. We drove through the narrow winding streets, bordered by graceful wood-balconied houses and ornate Venetian monuments from the time of Venetian rule. At tables outside the tabernas, old men sat smoking the long-stemmed chibouks, a custom acquired during the years of Ottoman rule. They stared at us somberly as we passed.

The following day we traveled the coastal highway east from Rethymnon to Iraklion, the capitol of the island and Crete's most populous city. The dusky faces of many of the inhabitants stemmed from the occupation of Arabs and Turks who in earlier centuries ruled Crete. Iraklion had suffered severely in WWII when most of the old Venetian and Turkish town was destroyed by bombings from the air.

Above the teeming streets of Iraklion, clogged with cars and carts, loomed the majestic Fortinago Bastion, where Nikos Kazantzakis, the greatest of the modern Greeks, was buried.

I had been looking forward eagerly to visiting the legendary Cretan's grave after reading his magnificent books. His novels, travel essays and poetry had provided me insight into the Greek soul and spirit. More than any other human being, Kazantzakis had inspired me in my own writing.

Looming as inanimate sentries around his grave stood three huge boulders depicting the three regions of the island. At the head of his grave was a stark, rough-hewn wooden cross without any name, date of birth or date of death. Only the moving inscription, "I hope for nothing, I fear nothing, I am free."

The day I visited, a score of young people sat alone or in small groups on stones or cross-legged on the ground around the grave. There were Oriental boys and dark-skinned girls. There were American girls and American youths, carrying backpacks and wearing baseball baps inscribed with the names of the Brooklyn Dodgers and the

New York Giants. Many held open books in their laps and were reading aloud to others.

A Greek groundskeeper whose responsibility was to look after the grave told me that throughout the seasons of the year, young people came from across the world to pay homage to the great Cretan poet. They would eat their lunches and read his books beside the grave.

"The master's work, you know, has been translated into fifty languages," the groundskeeper reminded me gravely. He slowly and reverently made his cross. "May God keep his memory eternal."

On still another visit I made with Diana and our sons during the summer a few years later, we sailed the Greek islands on an Epirotiki cruise ship called the *Jason*. Lawrence Durrell, a fervent Philhellene spoke of sailing the Greek islands as one of the world's great joys. A week of such travel confirmed that truth for us, as well.

We harbored at Rhodes with its sumptuous gardens and white-washed seaside towns. We rode donkeys up the cliffs of Santorini, donkeys that legend had it were inhabited by the souls of sinners whose bleak destiny was to carry overfed tourists up and down the mountain. From the highest peak of that island, the village of Thera, one could glimpse the horizons of the world.

From Santorini we sailed to the sacred island of Delos, uninhabited except for a caretaker looking after a row of majestic lion statues. From Delos we sailed to Mykonos, playground of young tourists from around the world. We saw hordes of them lined up outside the American Express office hoping for a check from home.

From the Greek islands, we sailed through the Bosporus into the harbor at Istanbul, the ancient city Greeks still call Constantinople, once heart of the great civilization known as Byzantium. My memories of that historic city were of teeming crowds clogging the streets. There were automobiles of assorted makes and models, their passage slowed and restricted by the pace of 'hamali,' human beasts of burden, men walking in the streets carrying great boxes and bundles perched on their heads.

Looming over Istanbul were the two venerable temples, the lovely Blue Mosque and the majestic Hagia Sophia, that timeless cathedral that once flourished as the heart of the great Byzantine Empire. As a result of the friction between Turk and Greek, the church had been reduced by the Turkish authorities to a desolate, neglected tomb.

The highlight of that visit was a meeting a group from our ship was permitted to meet with His Holiness, Patriarch Athenagoras, the spiritual leader of the Greek Orthodox Church around the world. A leviathan of a man standing at least six inches over six feet, he received us graciously. He had known my father as a young priest in America and he spoke kindly of him. As he embraced me, I could not resist the tears that came to my eyes.

One of the highlights of the travels to Greece during the 1970s, were my visits with Kimon Friar, the gifted poet and translator of many of the modern Greek poets. Friar had translated several of the works of Nikos Kazantzakis, including a masterful rendering in English of the epic *Odyssey, A Modern Sequel.* This 33,333-line poem by Kazantzakis resumed the adventures of the warrior Odysseus where the *Odyssey* of Homer ends, after Odysseus returns to Ithaca. To achieve the translation that critics called a "masterpiece," Friar had worked with Kazantzakis over a period of five years, including a number of meetings and a voluminous correspondence

For the *Athenian Magazine,* Friar had written a wonderful essay/ review of my Greek Revolution novel, *The Hour of the Bell.* I wrote him a note of gratitude that began our correspondence. On my next trip to Greece, I took a ferry from the mainland to visit Friar on the island of Evvia where he was living. We ate together, drank together, laughed and he shared with me stories of his working with the great poet.

On a later trip, soon after arriving at my hotel from the airport, I phoned Kimon at his apartment in Athens. He told me my timing was fortuitous since there was a party that evening at which the actress Melina Mercouri and her husband, the director Jules Dassin would be present. I tried to beg off citing my exhaustion from the long flight. Kimon insisted, and so I gave in and joined him.

The party was being held in the home of a renowned Greek novelist and poet, Antonis Samarakis. He was a buoyant, cordial host who brought me a glass of wine and a plate of appetizers after I'd been in the apartment for only minutes. Before I had finished the first glass of wine, I was introduced to Melina Mercouri and Jules Dassin. Mercouri was tall, lovely and regal with luminous eyes, already famous for her performance in the Dassin-directed film, *Never on Sunday*. There was a certain detachment about her, as if she were interred in her own thoughts and our introduction of only fleeting significance. By contrast, Dassin who was already fairly well drunk by the time I arrived, greeted me effusively. I felt an instant kinship to him. From the wine bottle he carried, he refilled my wine glass as well as his own and every few minutes, filled them again. The time Dassin had been drinking and my jet lag had us starting even.

In the following few hours, Dassin and I tried to out-drink one another. I'd say something, relate some experience, and his response remained the same, "Don't tell me that's true!" Then he'd erupt in a boisterous burst. "I don't believe it! You are making it up!" I'd reaffirm the truth of my statement, and he'd shake his head in emphatic rejection, laughing boisterously. At one point, rejecting my story, he leaned too far backwards and fell off his chair. Several of us hurried to pick him up while he just lay on the floor, continuing to laugh. All this time, I was conscious of Mercouri watching us, her eyes glinting with barbs of reproach.

Later in the evening, as we were all parting, Mercouri responded to my farewell with a censorious stare. "You and Jules," she said frostily, "should not be together."

One of the longest and most extensive of the Greek journeys I made came in the early 1970s, a trip I undertook to gain historical background for *The Hour of the Bell*, the novel on the Greek War of Independence I had contracted to write for the publishing house of Doubleday.

The regions of Greece I had visited up to that time had been limited to Athens, Crete and parts of the Peloponnesus.

In what became my most ambitious journey, my plan was to cover Greece from its sea-washed southern tip of the Mani, to the most northern mountain boundaries that adjoined Albania.

On several earlier trips I had utilized the driving services of an animated young Greek cab driver, Michalis Hadjaras, from the town of Nauplion. He had been a bus driver in the turbulent traffic of Athens, and then moved to Nauplion where he drove a taxi.

When I first arrived in Athens, in preparation for the journey I phoned him from my hotel. Some years later, while on a visit to Nauplion, another cab driver told me of being present when Michalis took my phone call. After speaking to me, Michalis turned haughtily to the other drivers and announced with gravitas, "That was my Uncle calling me from America, informing me to prepare for our epic journey!"

While waiting in Athens for Michalis to pick me up, I revisited the imposing Historical Museum, entering the spacious gallery that held paintings of the great warriors of the 1821 revolution. All the heroes I had read about in the histories and journals of the period, all were there. Kolokotronis, Karaiskakis, Boukouvalas and Marko Botzaris stared down at me from within their ornate frames. They were fierce-visaged, long-haired, eagle-eyed men, their brawny bodies bristling with bandoliers. They held long-barreled muskets, and pistols and daggers were visible in their sashes.

In that eerie moment, standing alone in the great gallery, I felt those warriors alive, gazing down at me with somber, judgmental faces. I felt their questioning how I had the audacity to attempt the enormous challenge of telling their story. What brashness to believe I could write boldly and honestly of that great rebellion to which they had devoted their lives!

In silence and humbly I offered them my pledge not to shame them.

That first day of our journey, in the car with Michalis, we drove the national highway departing from Athens and, after crossing the Gulf of Corinth, began heading south toward the Mani. After a day of driving, we stopped at Githion. I stayed in a room in a small hotel on the edge of the sea. By the light of a small lamp, I typed my day's notes on the small portable I carried. Afterwards, I tried to sleep despite the thunderous sound of waves crashing across the great rocks that bordered the shore.

The following day we drove to the legendary Mani, home of the warrior clans that had sacrificed so many lives to the cause of Greek Independence. Because of its massive mountain barriers, the Mani developed almost as a country separate from the rest of the Peloponnese.

When the Maniots were not fighting invaders they fought one another. Clans took refuge in great stone towers that lined the landscape and fought from there. From time to time a truce was declared when each side was allowed to bury its dead.

Another characteristic of the Mani were the stones. The landscape was littered with rocks and stones of all sizes. Fences and houses were built of stone and stone walkways lined the path into houses.

From the Mani we drove west to the city of Kalamata staying in an old hotel whose corridors smelled as musty as a mausoleum. The small closet-sized toilet next to my room had a basin stained with layers of rust. The compound was serviced by an old overhead box labeled with the imposing name of Niagara. Despite that reassuring appellation, when the chain was pulled, only a tiny trickle of water ensued.

On the third day we drove into the city of Patras on the Gulf of Patras. The following morning we'd take the car ferry across the gulf and begin our journey north into Epirus.

I had already been in Greece a week, and that night in Patras, I lay in bed in my hotel room that overlooked the harbor. Sights and sounds I had experienced during the day teemed in my mind and rendered me sleepless. Across the darkness, the plaintive wail of a ferry arriving from the Italian city of Brindisi evoked a nostalgia that made me think of home, Diana, and our sons.

The following morning we crossed the Gulf of Patras by car ferry, disembarking at Missolonghi where noble Lord Byron died fighting for Greek freedom. We visited the Garden of the Heroes with the tombs and ornate gravestones of the warriors of 1821.

Later that afternoon, traveling further north, we entered the old city of Ioannina where in the early nineteenth century, the cruel sultan Ali Pasha ruled. His own mini-revolt against the sultan in Constantinople afforded the Greeks the opportunity to launch their own revolt.

When we visited the cemetery where Ali Pasha was buried, with a passion and loathing undiminished almost two hundred years after the tyrant's reign, I witnessed a pair of young Greeks stamping and spitting on Ali Pasha's grave.

Then, grateful for the skilled hands and alert eyes of Michalis at the wheel of our vehicle, we began our journey into the austere and precipitous mountains of Epirus. After a morning of ascending higher and higher among the lofty crags, our first stop was in the mountain village of Metzovos. Around us the slopes and peaks looming above the village houses were shrouded in snow, the tree limbs sagging under their glazings of frost. That was the first snow I had ever seen anywhere in Greece.

Inside the village taberna, we sipped cups of steaming black coffee to warm our chilled bones. In a corner old men bundled in coats huddled around a small wood-burning stove. The air in the taberna hung thick with spirals of smoke. A few men smoked pipes and others puffed on the long-stemmed chibouks.

"Apo pou eisai?" "Where are you from?" I was asked several times in Greek.

"America," I answered.

"Ah, A-me-ri-kee," the old men spoke with reverence in their voices.

Other old men repeated the sacred word, and, for an instant, puffed more urgently on their pipes.

We resumed our journey, driving a spiraling road along the steep and hazardous roads of Epirus. Beyond the edges of the unrailed roadway, my stomach churning, I caught glimpses of valleys and farmlands thousands of feet below. Only the skilled hands of Michalis kept his sturdy little Opel firmly on the road.

At one point we picked up a highway worker stranded when his truck broke down. He huddled in the front seat beside Michalis. Very quickly it became evident the man had a virulent body odor as if he hadn't bathed in weeks. Until we dropped him off at a way station further up the mountain, Mihalis drove with his body pressed against the door and his head hanging out his open window.

Higher into the mountains we ascended to Kalabaka with its monasteries of the Meteora suspended in the sky. These monasteries had originally been built on the peaks of towering rocks by the monks as a refuge against the robber bands that roamed Greece. Trying to control my fear, I was hauled by basket and ropes up the side of the mountain to one of the monasteries.

I asked the monk who was my companion in the basket (riding with me to reassure me) how often they replaced the ropes. Although he had probably made that trip a number of times he looked as terrified as I felt.

"The Lord does not inform us when he wishes them to break," he said.

Inside the monastery, an aged monk greeted me warmly, and told me I was his first visitor in a year. Another old monk brought me a glass of wine and a few *paximadia*.

The view from the windows of that monastery in the sky was awesome, a scarlet-streaked and blue horizon layered upon still another multicolored horizon. The monk who seemed delighted at having a visitor told me the monastery that had once housed a hundred monks of their order, had only three remaining.

"What will happen when you three are gone?" I asked.

"Then the wind will say prayers," the old monk laughed, exposing a row of discolored and decaying teeth.

From Meteora, we resumed our journey, turning south along the highway once again, leaving behind snow and cold and entering green, flourishing farmlands. We traveled through the coastal cities of Larissa and Lamia and then, finally, after almost two weeks of traveling, we returned to Athens and I made plans to fly home.

In 1975, a year after the island of Cyprus had been ripped in half by the invasion of the Turkish armies, I went to Cyprus on a reporting assignment from the *New York Times*. The effects of the brief but brutal war could be seen in the faces of sorrowing villagers who had been driven from their homes in the northern part of the island. Many had been settled in newly erected refugee camps, tent settlements in which each family carried its own story of misery and loss.

A young Cypriot I spoke to told me that his father did nothing all day long but sit staring toward the northern part of the island.

"His farm is back there," the son explained. "Losing it was like ending his life. I fear he will die soon of a broken heart."

I was one of the first of about a dozen journalists in Cyprus at the time, allowed to cross the Green Line that divided the island between Greek and Turkish zones. A Turkish administrator was assigned to me as a guide and as a protector. I was a journalist with a letter of authorization from the *New York Times* but I also bore an unmistakably Greek name traveling in an area still inflamed by the recent war.

I visited Turkish villages and heard from the lips of old Turkish men who spoke fluent Greek, their stories of tyrannies imposed on them by the Greeks. While none of these indignities that included wanton destruction of their crops and the closing of water supplies to their villages warranted an army's invasion, their stories were poignant and their suffering real.

On that visit, with a dozen journalists from around the world also waiting to interview the island's legendary Archbishop Makarios, my Greek heritage gained me that privilege. Thanks to the assistance of the archbishop's administrative assistant, Patroclus Stavrou, I was allowed a brief visit with Archbishop Makarios.

The archbishop was a tall imposing man clad in his long black cassock, who was also president of the island. He had survived several assassination attempts only to be recently struck by a lethal heart attack from which he was slowly recovering. As I walked to our meeting, in a room adjoining his chambers, I saw a white-coated medical attendant sitting beside a tank of oxygen.

The archbishop spoke plaintively of his ordeal. "For so many years I guarded myself against our enemies, escaping several of their efforts to kill me. But the attack I never expected and had no way of defending came from within my own body." He placed his fingers pensively on his black cassock above his heart.

A few months later, back in the U.S. I heard the news of the archbishop's death.

There were other journeys I made alone or with Diana to lands besides Greece and Crete. On one trip we flew Air France into Paris. We landed in the cavernous De Gaulle Airport and seemed to walk miles before we could leave the terminal. We traveled by taxi into the heart of that sparkling city. In late afternoon, sitting in a sidewalk café similar to those where Hemingway once lingered, we listened to the voices of Parisians flinging vowels and consonants of their mellifluent language into the air.

We visited the majestic galleries of the Louvre and the Musée d' Orsay. We walked past the Cathedral of Notre Dame, drove around the Eiffel Tower, and sat on a grassy knoll alongside the Seine where lumbering barges seemed to be perched motionless on the surface of the water.

From Paris we traveled to Munich in Germany with its venerable museums and libraries, found the Germans a courteous, orderly people. We visited the Olympic stadium where the Israeli athletes had been murdered. From that city, I will not forget the decorous and gracious manager of our hotel on Bahnhoffstrasse Street, greeting me each morning with a thickly accented, "Gut dayyyy, Herr Pe-tra-kees!"

We traveled north from Germany to Copenhagen in Denmark, a city of bazaars and parks teeming with the vibrant beauty of blonde Danish girls and blond Danish youths, all moving through the streets less in a walk than in a quick, supple dance.

Walking alone one afternoon through a lovely Copenhagen park, I passed groups of young people lounging and picnicking on the grassy knolls. After a few moments I realized that a number of the lovely girls were either bare-breasted or fully naked. Fearing I would be seen as a lecherous Yankee creep peeping at these bare-breasted and bare-thighed beauties, I tried to flee the park only to find myself lost, wandering the same paths, trying to keep my eyes on the walk before me.

One of the stellar events of that visit was our spending opening night at Tivoli Gardens in Copenhagen, one of the world's great amusement parks. Beneath the beams of thousands of overhead lights. There were ferris wheels and merry-go-rounds, and a hundred booths and stalls, stocked with multiple mementoes to carry home.

We crossed the channel to England, emerging from our plane at Heathrow Airport to the area where the black hansom cabs awaited travelers. (On one of our earlier trips, before we learned the art of packing sparely for travel, a half dozen of those hansom taxi drivers rejected us as passengers because of the amount of our luggage. I remember our sense of isolation and mortification as we stood on the curb like pariahs; our eight pieces of luggage piled around us while other people passed us in silent rebuke and entered cabs.)

We traveled from Heathrow into fabled London with its monuments to the historic past. Trafalgar Square, the Tower of London, gloomy Westminster Abbey shrouding the tombs of venerable English poets. As with previous visits, I spent almost a full day browsing among the literary treasures of the British Museum.

We drove into the English countryside with its small villages and sprawling hills. The dining halls of the University at Oxford haunted by the centuries old tread of countless young men, the walls bearing plaques on which were embedded the names of young Englishmen killed in a succession of the Empire's wars. There was a wall dedicated to the young German students who had attended Oxford at the time of the war and had died fighting for their own country.

We flew from England to Ireland to be hurled into the buoyancy of the pubs in Joyce's Dublin, the bustle of Grafton Street, Trinity College and a multitudinous array of churches. Then a brief crossing from Ireland to Scotland with its glens and the castles of Edinburgh and Glasgow, inhabited by the ghosts of Scottish kings.

Our driver, Angus, was from Glasgow and our young tour guide Mary Melton was from Edinburgh. For the two days of our journey, they joked and teased one another on the superior merits of their respective cities.

During another trip I made alone, I traveled across Israel, standing before the Wailing Wall in Jerusalem, old black-cloaked Orthodox Hassidim standing beside me, their upper bodies weaving back and forth as they fervently prayed. I was driven around that small ancient country, by my driver and guide, Eli Spector. We viewed the Sea of Galilee at twilight and the tomb of the Nativity in Bethlehem. We climbed Masada and, at the highest peak, encountered a pervasive mist concealing the ghosts of Roman armies that had once besieged the Israelites.

In a border kibbutz, I descended into the underground bunkers where the children slept at night as a haven from the rocket fire that came nightly from Lebanon.

A young girl, a great grand-niece of Israel's founder, David Ben-Gurion, and who I was told wished to be a writer was brought to meet me. When I asked what she wrote about, she answered quietly, "I write about people who live each day and night in fear."

In the mid-1990s, working on a history of the electronic giant, Motorola, Diana and I made visits to the company's offices and plants in Asia. That was a strange, mesmerizing world where we moved among the exceedingly courteous, yet enigmatic peoples of Japan, Korea and Malaysia. We participated in the ritualistic ceremonies that marked greetings and farewells. All around us were the ornate temples, the multiple statues of Buddha. We inhaled the scents of what were to us strange, exotic foods. We crossed streets warily, dodging the cyclists whipping their motorbikes in and out among the swarm of cars.

In still other cities, we witnessed the quiet, orderly movement of people in the streets of Hong Kong; the bewitching beauty of young women in Singapore, skirts cut in long slits to expose their slender silken-clad thighs.

As I move now through the bazaars of memory, I recall the plays, dramas and musicals we've seen in those cities we visited around the world. Plays of Anton Chekhov, Henrik Ibsen, Eugene O'Neill, Samuel Beckett, Tennessee Williams, Arthur Miller and a score of others. Concerts and symphonies, and sitting in the audience listening to the great solo artists, Itzhak Perlman, Luciano Pavarotti, Andreas Bocelli, Gregor Piatigorsky, Andrés Segovia.

Intertwined with all the journeys and spanning every day, week and month, were the links of friendship. A poet has written that life without a friend is death without a witness. We have borne such witness hundreds of times and hundreds of men and women have borne witness for us. With these friends we have shared the milestone events of weddings and baptisms, the holidays of Easter, Thanksgiving, Christmas, birthdays, baptisms and weddings. A small book would be needed to list all their names.

Finally, in more recent years, the frequency of funerals, as many of these treasured old friends age with us, grow ill and die. But with each death we are once again reminded to evaluate the magnitude and majesty of the journey that is life, that luminous interval we are granted from the moment of our birth until the instant of our death.

NOW, HAVING ATTEMPTED to make up for the omissions in the manuscript, I reenter the old troubadour's song that began this chapter and revisit his slow, ritualistic dance. My own arms and legs grown brittle, my shoulders stooped, sounds for me grown fainter, images blurred, I understand him now in a way I could not fully understand him then. We are joined once more, a pair of old men singing, dancing and writing their life's journeys. Until all our music, song and dance, those harmonies and images that words can fashion, all drift, finally, into silence.